The
Salvadoran
Americans

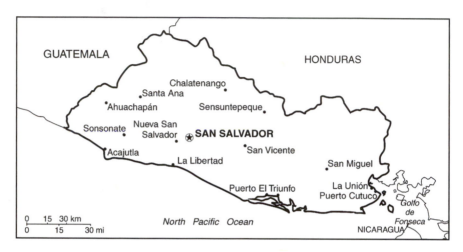

El Salvador.

The
Salvadoran
Americans

Carlos B. Cordova

THE NEW AMERICANS
Ronald H. Bayor, Series Editor

GREENWOOD PRESS
Westport, Connecticut • London

Library of Congress Cataloging-in-Publication Data

Cordova, Carlos B.
  The Salvadoran Americans / Carlos B. Cordova.
      p. cm. — (The New Americans, ISSN 1092–6364)
  Includes bibliographical references and index.
  ISBN 0–313–32306–2 (alk. paper)
  1. Salvadoran Americans. 2. Salvadoran Americans—Social conditions. 3. Immigrants—United States—Social conditions. 4. El Salvador—Emigration and immigration. 5. United States—Emigration and immigration. I. Title. II. Series: New Americans (Westport, Conn.)
E184.S15C67   2005
305.868'7284073—dc22   2005020463

British Library Cataloguing in Publication Data is available.

Library of Congress Catalog Card Number: 2005020463
ISBN: 0–313–32306–2
ISSN: 1092–6364

First published in 2005

Greenwood Press, 88 Post Road West, Westport, CT 06881
An imprint of Greenwood Publishing Group, Inc.
www.greenwood.com

Printed in the United States of America

The paper used in this book complies with the Permanent Paper Standard issued by the National Information Standards Organization (Z39.48–1984).

10 9 8 7 6 5 4 3 2 1

Contents

PART III   ADJUSTMENT AND ADAPTATION

Tables

Series Foreword

Oscar Handlin, a prominent historian, once wrote, "I thought to write a history of the immigrants in America. Then I discovered that the immigrants were American history." The United States has always been a nation of nations where people from every region of the world have come to begin a new life. Other countries such as Canada, Argentina, and Australia also have had substantial immigration, but the United States is still unique in the diversity of nationalities and the great numbers of migrating people who have come to its shores.

Who are these immigrants? Why did they decide to come? How well have they adjusted to this new land? What has been the reaction to them? These are some of the questions the books in this "New Americans" series seek to answer. There have been many studies about earlier waves of immigrants— e.g., the English, Irish, Germans, Jews, Italians, and Poles—but relatively little has been written about the newer groups—those arriving in the last thirty years, since the passage of a new immigration law in 1965. This series is designed to correct that situation and to introduce these groups to the rest of America.

Each book in this series discusses one of these groups, and each is written by an expert on those immigrants. The volumes cover the new migration from primarily Asia, Latin America, and the Caribbean, including the Koreans, Cambodians, Filipinos, Vietnamese, South Asians such as Indians and Pakistanis, Chinese from both China and Taiwan, Haitians, Jamaicans, Cubans, Dominicans, Mexicans, Puerto Ricans (even though they are already U.S. citizens), and Jews from the former Soviet Union. Although some of these people, such as Jews, have been in America since colonial times, this series concentrates on their recent migrations, and thereby offers its unique contribution.

These volumes are designed for high school and general readers who want to learn more about their new neighbors. Each author has provided information about the land of origin, its history and culture, the reasons for migrating, and the ethnic culture as it began to adjust to American life. Readers will find fascinating details on religion, politics, foods, festivals, gender roles, employment trends, and general community life. They will learn how Vietnamese immigrants differ from Cuban immigrants and, yet, how they are also alike in many ways. Each book is arranged to offer an in-depth look at the particular immigrant group but also to enable readers to compare one group with the other. The volumes also contain brief biographical profiles of notable individuals, tables noting each group's immigration, and a short bibliography of readily available books and articles for further reading. Most contain a glossary of foreign words and phrases.

Students and others who read these volumes will secure a better understanding of the age-old questions of "who is an American" and "how does the assimilation process work?" Similar to their nineteenth- and early-twentieth-century forebears, many Americans today doubt the value of immigration and fear the influx of individuals who look and sound different from those who had come earlier. If comparable books had been written one hundred years ago they would have done much to help dispel readers' unwarranted fears of the newcomers. Nobody today would question, for example, the role of those of Irish or Italian ancestry as Americans; yet, this was a serious issue in our history and a source of great conflict. It is time to look at our recent arrivals, to understand their history and culture, their skills, their place in the United States, and their hopes and dreams as Americans.

The United States is a vastly different country than it was at the beginning of the twentieth century. The economy has shifted away from industrial jobs; the civil rights movement has changed minority-majority relations and, along with the women's movement, brought more people into the economic mainstream. Yet one aspect of American life remains strikingly similar—we are still the world's main immigrant receiving nation and as in every period of American history, we are still a nation of immigrants. It is essential that we attempt to learn about and understand this long-term process of migration and assimilation.

Ronald H. Bayor
Georgia Institute of Technology

Acknowledgments

As a Salvadoran living in the United States since 1965, I have been a witness and an active participant in the many changes experienced by Salvadoran communities in this country. Since the early 1970s, I was inspired by the Salvadoran immigrant experience in California, and it was then that I decided to dedicate my professional and academic life to the study and research of Central American cultures and experiences as they were developing throughout many U.S. regions.

I am indebted to all the Central American immigrants that participated in the numerous research projects that I have been involved in over the years, for their cooperation and sincerity in providing me with the narratives of their life experiences in Central America as well as their journey and resettlement in the United States. This book is dedicated to them.

I would like to express my gratitude to many individuals and institutions that have provided me with the financial, logistical, and emotional support to pursue my research goals for three decades. I am extending sincere words of appreciation to the College of Ethnic Studies and the Cesar Chavez Institute for Public Policy at San Francisco State University for the sabbatical leave awards that allowed me the opportunity to fully dedicate myself to writing this book during 2003–2004. I would like to extend words of appreciation to my colleagues at San Francisco State University who encouraged and supported me over the years in my research efforts, some of them are Carlos Baron, Dr. Jose Cuellar, Dr. Rudy Busby, and the late Dr. Ted Murguia who mentored me for many years. I am also grateful to the Ford Foundation and the North-South Center at the University of Miami for helping to fund the research on Salvadorans and Guatemalans in San Francisco and Los Angeles. These research experiences during the 1990s were a collaborative effort that I carried out with Nora Hamilton, Norma Chinchilla, and Susanne Jonas, and I am grateful for their support during those years of extensive fieldwork.

I also extend words of appreciation to the Vesper Society in Oakland, California, and to Sylvia Rosales-Fike who took the leadership in developing the Central American Strategic Planning Task Force, empowering a group of Salvadoran activists with the responsibilities of analyzing the experiences of Salvadoran immigrant populations in a number of U.S. cities in the mid-1990s. Special thanks to Roberto Lovato, Oscar Chacón, Mauricio Alarcón, Yvonne Rivera, and Nicolás Avelar. That was an invaluable experience that allowed me to get an insider's perspective in the lives of many Salvadorans and provided me with a critical understanding of the local communities in San Francisco, Los Angeles, Houston, New York, New Jersey, Boston, Washington, D.C., and other urban centers.

I would like to thank Mara E. Rosales and my children, Alexis and Xochitl, for their support while I had to travel and spend long hours in the field conducting research and writing. And to my parents, sisters, brothers, cousins, and all my relatives in the United States who were my initial inspiration for studying the Salvadoran realities in the United States. I extend special appreciation to Tania Lisa Llambelis for her constant support and encouragement during the months that I spent writing this book. My thankfulness also goes to Yemayá, Oshún, and Changó for giving me the spiritual fortitude to keep the research going during long and difficult periods in my life. Omío Yemayá! Cari Ye Yeo! Kawo Sile Changó!

Thank you so much, I could not have done it without all of you.

PART I

BACKGROUND

1

El Salvador, the Land of Origin

GEOGRAPHY

El Salvador is the smallest country in Central and Latin America. Because of the small size of its territory, the great Chilean poet Gabriela Mistral baptized it as "El Pulgarcito de America" or the Tom Thumb of the Americas. The country is also known as the land of lakes and volcanoes.

El Salvador has an area of 8,124 square miles, which is approximately the size of Massachusetts. Its neighbors are Guatemala to the west and north; Honduras to the east and north; and Nicaragua across the Gulf of Fonseca. To the south is the Pacific Ocean as a natural boundary. El Salvador is approximately 160 miles long from east to west and about 60 miles wide from the Pacific Ocean to the Honduras border. The coastline is approximately 186 miles long. The Pacific coast region has a hot tropical climate, and then the terrain rises to a cooler region characterized by valleys and volcanoes. The northern region, which lies closer to Honduras, also has many volcanoes and crater lakes, but the north has a more temperate climate than the coastal areas near the Pacific Ocean.

Until recently, El Salvador was known to have a lush tropical forest, but in recent decades the country has experienced a high level of deforestation, soil erosion, water pollution, soil contamination from disposal of toxic waste, and environmental degradation, which in turn have had a serious impact on the climate as well as the human environment. In addition, the Civil War of the 1980's contributed a great deal to the environmental destruction and contamination of the fertile valleys and mountainous regions. The "scorch the earth" tactics and the use of napalm and white phosphorous bombs during the war had a serious impact on the countryside. Another factor that contributed to deforestation and the destruction of the rich soil in the coastal valleys was the intensified agricultural practices in huge farms that were dedicated to the cultivation of cotton and sugar cane. Approximately 39 percent of the land is used for agricultural purposes. The extensive and uncontrolled use of pesticides, herbicides, and irrigation ended up destroying many rich agricultural areas to the point that large portions had to be abandoned and left idle for many years. Chemicals and human waste have contaminated many water resources all over the country.

The climate is characterized by two seasons: the rainy season takes place from May to October, and the dry season from November to April. The dry season has high temperatures and dusty winds whereas tropical storms are common and tropical hurricanes a possibility during the rainy seasons. With its many volcanoes, the country is frequently affected by strong and destructive earthquakes and frequent volcanic activity. The capital city, San Salvador, has been destroyed by earthquakes throughout its history and is located in the region known as the Valley of the Hammocks because of its frequent shakes and earthquakes.

DEMOGRAPHICS

The 2003 population of El Salvador was estimated to be 6,470,379 persons. It is also estimated that at least another 2 million Salvadorans live outside the country. Approximately 37 percent of the Salvadoran population is younger than 14 years of age, and about 60 percent of the population is between the ages of 15 and 64. Only 5 percent of the population is older than 65 years of age. The country experiences a high rate of infant mortality with about 27 deaths per 1,000 live births. The life expectancy at birth in El Salvador is approximately 70 years; 67 years for males and 74 years for females. The Salvadoran government official sources state that the ethnic makeup of the population is 90 percent mestizo, which is a racial mixture of Spanish and indigenous peoples; 9 percent white or European; and only 1 percent Indian. Other ethnic groups that are part of the Salvadoran society include Arabs, Palestinians, and Jews. There is also a significant Chinese community. In the Salvadoran presidential elections of 2004 the top two candidates were Salvadorans of Palestinian origin.

The country is divided into 14 departments or states, and the capital is San Salvador. In recent years, as a result of the large numbers of Salvadorans who have left the country, a new concept has been developed in regards to the structure of the nation. A 15th and new department, "el Departamento Quince," has been created by the Salvadoran media and supported by the Salvadoran government, as an abstract concept to include Salvadorans who live abroad throughout the migration diasporas but continue to contribute to the social, economic, political, and cultural life of the country. Salvadorans living abroad are referring to as "Hermanos Lejanos"—the brothers that live far away. As one drives from the Comalapa International Airport into San Salvador, there is the huge monument of the "Hermanos Lejanos," which was erected to honor those who left the country but continue to contribute to the local economies by sending monetary remittances to their families.

LANGUAGE AND LITERACY

Spanish is the official language of El Salvador, but some of the indigenous peoples also speak Nahuat, the ancient language spoken in the area before the arrival of the Spaniards. The official Salvadoran government statistics state that 80 percent of the population is able to read and write. The official definition of literacy is a person age 10 and older that can read and write. But in reality under this definition, there are many persons that are functional illiterates.

HISTORY

The Central American region where El Salvador is located has a long history of cultural development as well as social unrest. The land is rich and highly suitable for intensified agricultural activity; therefore throughout the centuries many different groups have been interested in colonizing it. In pre-Hispanic times the area was populated and controlled by various groups arriving from Mexico, Guatemala, and Honduras. Cultural groups such as the Toltecs, the Mayas, and the Aztecs extended their economic, social, and cultural influences throughout the area as they colonized it and use the natural resources found there.

The contemporary indigenous peoples of El Salvador still show many elements of the pre-Hispanic cultures such as their language, known as Nahuat; their social organization, which is based on the Aztec and Mayan social systems; as well as their religious and spiritual traditions. One important social institution that still remains from pre-Hispanic times is the *Chinamit* or *Calpulli,* as it was called in Central Mexico. The *Chinamit* is the organization led by the Indian elders who are in charge of communal land distribution, conflict resolution, and social organization in Central American indigenous societies. It is a government that is parallel to the national government, and many indigenous peoples gave more respect and allegiance to the *chinamit* than to the nation-state.

The present-day Pipil culture in El Salvador has its roots in ancient Mexico, as a result of the large migrations of Toltecs and other ethnic groups that arrived from central and southern Mexico around 400 C.E. while attempting to escape the new social order that was being imposed by the militaristic societies that had taken over many city-states throughout central Mexico. The new military empire demanded taxes and victims to be sacrificed to their gods of War; therefore, large segments of the central Mexican population migrated south to the Central American region seeking refuge and a new place to live. The new arrivals mixed with the native populations and influenced the region by spreading their language, culture, religion, and social organization. This is one of the main reasons why El Salvador has such strong Mexican elements in its present cultural and religious traditions. The Mexican influences may be observed in the names of towns and cities that are repeated from their original places in Mexico. It is also common to see the names of Mexican geographical locations and formations repeated as one follows the migration routes from central Mexico to the furthest places of the Central American region.

With the arrival of the Spanish conquistadores, the Central American indigenous societies experienced dramatic changes. The Spanish conquest of Central America caused an immediate collapse of the ancient indigenous social systems and decimated much of the population as a result of the wars of conquest, slavery, forced labor, and the introduction of new diseases from Europe, against which the indigenous peoples had no biological resistance. During the early years of the conquest of Central America, the indigenous population was devastated by diseases such as smallpox, the bubonic plague, and other epidemics that had plagued Europe for a number of centuries. It is estimated that approximately 80 percent of the entire population of Central America was killed by the new illnesses and epidemics, as well as by the abuse from the dehumanizing system of slavery.

The Spanish conquistadores had one main interest in the conquest and colonization of the Americas: to acquire large amounts of gold, which in turn would bring them power and wealth in the European courts. But Central America lacked the great gold resources found in Peru or the silver found in Mexico; therefore, the colonizers turned to forced labor and the exportation of agriculture in order to exploit the local resources in El Salvador and the rest of Central America. Indian people and newly imported Africans were forced into a ruthless system of slavery that was used to cultivate agricultural crops which were exported to Europe and would bring wealth to the new colonies. Some of these export crops included tobacco, indigo, cochineal, and balsam. The use of tobacco became quite popular throughout the royal courts in Spain and the rest of Europe, to such an extent that royalty adopted a traditional practice of the Mayans of placing a small pipe on their headdresses as a sign of distinction. Indigo and cochineal were popular dyes used in textiles. Indigo is a blue dye and cochineal is a scarlet dye, and their use became popular in Europe and later in the British colonies of the Americas. Cochineal was used in the red coats worn by the British soldiers, and Indigo was later used in the blue coats worn in the British colonies in the Americas during the Revolutionary Wars.

The colonial economic system was founded on a system of slavery that segregated the natives from the colonizers and created a new social structure based on racial mixture known as castes. The more European blood that people had in their veins, the higher their position in the social structure and the more opportunities, both financial and political, that were available to them. The Spanish-born colonizers were known as the "Peninsulares" because they had the "divine privilege" of having been born in the Iberian Peninsula.

The Indian and African slaves were at the lower levels of the social scale. They were forced to live in segregated communities where no Europeans or people of mixed Spanish and Indian blood, known as *mestizos,* were allowed to reside. Indians were allowed to work only in communal land plots where traditional Indian agricultural crops used for internal consumption were being produced. This practice of allowing the communal indigenous labor to continue became the foundation for the internal and local economies of the colonial society and was responsible for the cultivation of corn, beans, squashes, tomatoes, and many other crops that historically had been part of the local diet.

The export agricultural system was designed to bring a limited amount of wealth to the Central American colonies while paying high taxes to the Spanish Crown. As a result, and following the footsteps of the revolutionary movements in other parts of the American continent, Central American revolutionaries began to organize an independence movement from Spain. This was a movement led by an aspiring social class known as the *Criollos* or creoles, who were the full-blooded children of Spaniards but were not allowed to hold the most important positions in the political and economic power of the colonial society because they had been born in the American continent. The leadership of this revolutionary movement included low-level and mid-ranking members of the military and the Catholic Church.

The Colonial society in Central American had been somewhat independent from Mexico, where the seat of the Viceroyalty of New Spain was located. After independence from Spain was achieved on September 15, 1821, the Mexican and the Central American conservatives incorporated Central America into the Mexican empire of Agustín Iturbide without any major opposition. This political move was part of the plan of the conservative landowners, aristocrats, and civil and religious leaders in Guatemala to create an independent society based on the feudal colonial economic and political system left by the Spaniards in the Americas.

On November 23, 1822, the province of San Salvador decided to seek annexation to the United States as the means to stop the process of annexation to Mexico. The Guatemalan department of Chiapas was the first Central American province to separate from Central America and was officially annexed to Mexico. Chiapas had been part of Guatemala since pre-Hispanic times. When the Empire of Iturbide fell, José Cecilio del Valle, the liberal Central American representative in Washington, nullified the annexation of San Salvador to the United States.

On June 24, 1823, the First Congress of Central America declared that the provinces would unite and be called the "Provincias Unidas de Centro América," the United Provinces of Central America. They adopted a system of government based on the federal system of the United States. The 50 years after independence were chaotic for the Central American Liberals and became known as the "Period of Anarchy," which was marked by constant civil wars in the region. It was fought between the Liberals and the Conservatives.

The Federalists modeled their reformist platform around a strategy to make Central America a main exporting region of raw materials to the industrializing countries of Europe. The conservatives wanted the status quo of the colonial period. The wars lasted for more than two decades, destroying the economy and creating social chaos. The armies caused great destruction in the plantations *(haciendas)* and in the trade of the most important cash crops.

By 1865, the United Provinces disbanded into the five countries that presently make up the Central American region, and a group of very powerful and wealthy conservative landowners began to share the economic and political power in the area. They shared the political power among their own family members up until 1930 and became known as the "oligarchic families" in El Salvador. They nationalized Indian lands and began the forced cultivation of coffee as an export crop. They developed large coffee plantations that they eventually acquired from the government at very low prices. This was the beginning of economic dependency on a single agricultural crop.

Francisco Dueñas is known as the father of the oligarchy. During the early years of conservative oligarchic rule, the government of El Salvador tried to balance the economic crisis brought about by the period of anarchy. The first measure was to relieve the indigo monoculture that had been decaying for many decades. New crops were being considered as export crops, such as cacao, balsam, gum, coffee, tobacco, agave fiber, vanilla beans, and wheat. The growers of these preferred crops were exempt from taxation and their workers were exempt from military service.

During the late 1800s, the Indian communal land rights were respected, and the *Ejidos* played an important part in this period. The Indian leaders were required to produce maps so as to have better control of the communal lands. The institution of the *Ejido (Chinamit)* was similar to the ancestral concepts of land tenure. The main difference was that the Indian community was not in charge of land distribution; instead, the municipal government owned the land and lent parcels to those who needed it for planting a small orchard, collecting firewood, or grazing a few animals. The *Ejido* system has disappeared in El Salvador.

The government followed a political platform that would support its own interests, which would be justified with the new imported economic theories of laissez-faire—a doctrine, policy, or ideal holding that government should not interfere with economic activity. It is assumed that the competition is capable of acting as the supreme regulator of the economy, preventing restrictions on trade or production and promoting efficiency and progress.

In El Salvador, the indigenous people suffered a great deal of repression in the late 1920s and early 1930s. The collapse of the world market had a serious impact on the Salvadoran economy, and in turn it affected the rural agricultural communities as well as indigenous culture and society. Coffee prices collapsed in the world market and the landowners decided not to harvest coffee. The agrarian society of El Salvador was collapsing and the farm workers *(campesinos)* were the ones to feel the direct effects of the economic depression. They were seasonal workers and had no money, food, or shelter. Hunger, then, created the perfect catalyst for revolution. The urban workers and the *campesinos* had organized to demand better living and working conditions, but the results were devastating for them, as their revolution was unsuccessful in 1932.

The social organization of indigenous peoples was structured around the Chinamit, their ancient communal system of land distribution known as the "Calpulli" or "Chinamit." Because of their communal social structure, the government labeled indigenous peoples and their leaders as communist, and a campaign of persecution was started against indigenous communities in El Salvador. The government created a wave of terror across the entire countryside; the rural people suffered the repressive search and destroy tactics used by the National Guard. The National Guard, led by General Maximiliano

Hernandez Martinez, was a new military institution that had been designed to protect the economic interests of the ruling families. Most people in the rural areas fit into the description of the suspects wanted by the government armed forces. Anybody who carried a machete, which was the traditional work tool and weapon used in the countryside, dressed as a *campesino* or in traditional indigenous clothing, had Indian features, or spoke the native Indian languages was captured and, without any trial, was executed by one of the many firing squads established by the National Guard. It is estimated that between 10,000 and 30,000 people were summarily executed in less than three weeks by the repressive military forces of the government.[1]

Since the 1932 revolution, most of the *campesinos* and indigenous peoples of El Salvador were forced to abandon many of their traditional ways, because of the systematic persecution and repression of the indigenous people by the National Guard. They were forced to stop speaking their native languages, forego their traditional dress styles, and hide their ritual practices and use of the ancient pre-Hispanic calendar. Presently, very few Indian people are willing to speak in their native language in front of strangers, and only a small number of Indian women still wear their traditional colorful dress particular to their community, while the men have almost completely lost that aspect of their traditional culture. When ritual is practiced, it is conducted in an atmosphere of secrecy and distrust of strangers.

This period marked the beginning of a new political experience in El Salvador. The military assumed a position of importance in the political life of the country. Military officers became the political representatives of the economic interests of the oligarchic families. This period was also important because the first significant number of Salvadorans begins to arrive in the United States to escape political persecution and the unrest that affected the region. Between 1932 and 1979, the military presidents controlled the political life of El Salvador, and militarism became part of the social fiber in Salvadoran politics. By the late 1970s many of the military governments had become repressive dictatorships that did not allow political dissent and subjected the Salvadoran population to political repression and human rights abuses.

During the 1950s and 1960s, the Salvadoran economy was concentrated in large-scale agricultural farms that cultivated cash crops for export. The best available lands in the coastal regions were dedicated to the cultivation of cotton, while most Salvadoran farm workers had difficulties in obtaining small plots of land to use for subsistence agriculture. By the 1970s the economic power of the elites had grown to high levels never seen before in the region.

THE SALVADORAN CIVIL WAR

The economic reality of Central America during the 1970s was very difficult, and in El Salvador the military governments and the oligarchic families had begun to deemphasize agricultural exports as the foundation of the Salvadoran economy. Therefore, the rural areas suffered from underemployment as few economic opportunities were available in the rural sector. This resulted in large numbers of Salvadorans being displaced in their rural communities and a large migration of unskilled agricultural people moving to the capitol seeking new employment opportunities.

The new economic emphasis was placed on foreign economic investments that were bringing a new supply of low paying jobs in urban factories and would give the local and foreign investors huge profits from the manufacture of products that would be sold in the U.S. markets. The 1970s were characterized by the development of "free economic zones," where transnational corporations would set up maquiladoras, assembly line factories that provided low wages to the workers while paying very low or no taxes to the government. This was a time when the wealth became even more concentrated in the hands of a few families. The impact of the new economic model brought a number of problems to the Central American countries. Workers toiled for low pay and no health or other types of benefits were provided to them. The capital became overcrowded, and new residential low-income communities were built in close proximity to the factories. Rural and urban workers began to organize and took to the streets to protest the working conditions and exploitation in the factories, and they were often met with violent, repressive actions on the part of the police.

The labor unions and worker organizations became highly organized and militant in their efforts to get positive results from their demands to the government. They organized massive labor strikes, took over land from the large landowners, demonstrated in the streets, and had peaceful marches that were dispersed violently by government forces.

On October 15, 1979, a group of young military officers interested in reforming the armed forces overthrew the military dictatorship of General Carlos Humberto Romero and put a civilian military junta in power. But the junta members were unable to stop the repression and realized that the military generals were really in control of the political life of the country. As the levels of political violence and repression rapidly increased, the junta appointed José Napoleón Duarte as President in December 1980. The junta was dissolved, the young progressive officers went into exile, and many of the civilians joined the Revolutionary Democratic Front. In 1984, Duarte was reelected President.

After the 1979 overthrow of the military government of General Romero, the military and police forces began to escalate the repression and the violence and resorted to the creation of para-military death squads that targeted for assassination the most important political activists and militants of the opposition. The death squads were organized by the top military officers and financed by civilians associated with the powerful economic oligarchic families. The death squads were led by off-duty military officers, and membership included off-duty members of the armed forces and police organizations, as well as right wing civilian organizations. Their main political targets were priests and lay preachers associated with the Liberation Theology movement that since the early 1960s had worked to renew the teachings of the Catholic Church while reinterpreting the gospel to address the social realities of the poor in this world. In El Salvador, a group of young Catholic priests began to take their social mission seriously and actively worked to change the socio-economic conditions of the rural and urban poor. They organized lay persons who were committed to work and organize among the poor, and charismatic bishops such as Monsignor Oscar Arnulfo Romero and other priests encouraged the calls for the government to develop progressive programs and modernize the country. These priests also worked with students in the upper class high schools as the means to provide these young people with a critical analysis of the social and political conditions experienced by the Salvadoran people from all different social classes. As a result, a number of social organizations were created such as Young Christian Students, Young Christian Workers, Young Christian Farm Workers, the Movement for Basic Education, and the first base ecclesial communities. The Salvadoran government and the military, as well as the wealthy Salvadoran class, considered these social movements as communist oriented and targeted their leadership for political persecution.

During this time, the death squads also targeted opposition political party leaders and activists, labor leaders, teachers, high school and university students and their families, as well as anyone associated with the emerging revolutionary organizations throughout the country. Members of the Salvadoran death squads would often wear plain clothes and make use of trucks or vans with tinted windows and without license plates. Sometimes victims were shot from passing cars, or taken from their homes, or off the streets, and their bodies were abandoned far from the scene of the crime. Bodies were thrown along roadsides, in full view of the public, or in trash dumps. Among the methods used by the death squads to intimidate their victims was the advertising of threats in the national press. Official government statements accusing individuals of

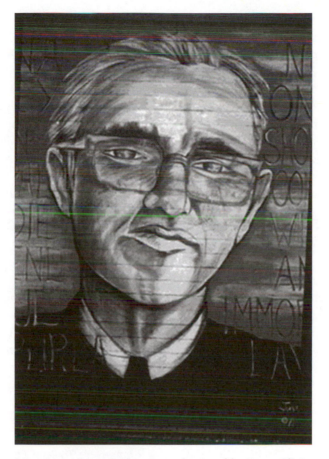

Monsignor Oscar Romero mural painted by Juana Alicia,
Balmy Alley, San Francisco, CA. Photo by Carlos Texca.

belonging to, sympathizing with, or acting with the Frente Farabundo Martí
para la Liberación Nacional (FMLN) guerrillas also gave a green light for death
squads to eliminate the branded person. Such statements were often interpreted
by human rights organizations in El Salvador as a death warrant.

During the 1980s, Salvadoran governments customarily claimed that death
squad activity and killings were the work of extremist groups operating beyond
government control. In a 1984 publication, Amnesty International concluded
that death squads were made up of regular police and military personnel, often
operating in plain clothes but under the orders of superior officers.[2]

Investigative reports conducted after the Civil War ended and based on
classified documents released by the Clinton Administration disclosed the

involvement of high-ranking members of the armed forces and of the Alianza Republicana Nacionalista political party (ARENA) in the planning and operation of death-squad activities in El Salvador through out the 1980s and into the 1990s. Moreover, documents from 1990 link such activities to top officials of the ARENA government and armed forces. The report describes how ARENA's paramilitary organization operated in coordination with a death squad comprised primarily of members of the National Police, and how the National Police would provide weapons to support ARENA paramilitary operations. ARENA often acted as an umbrella organization for a diversity of death squads, including those operating out of the security forces, to tie the work of these distinct paramilitary groups together under a unified political plan.[3]

The early 1980s were marked by an escalation of military repression, political assassinations, and large-scale violations of human rights in the civilian population. There were a number of massacres that killed hundreds of civilians in various parts of the country. Death squads targeted priests and religious leaders, and a death squad in San Salvador assassinated Archbishop Oscar Arnulfo Romero, who had taken a position against the military's use of violence against civilians while he was saying mass in a neighborhood church. Other victims were the leadership of the Revolutionary Democratic Front and large numbers of activists, teachers, union leaders and others who opposed the government. Estimates put the number of dead in 1981–82 to a figure close to 25,000 people. It was then that tens of thousands of Salvadorans fled the country in an attempt to escape the political violence and repression. It is in this context that approximately 600,000 farm workers became refugees inside their own country. Many others went to refugee camps in Honduras, Nicaragua, and Costa Rica. Another 800,000 Salvadorans went to Mexico, Venezuela, the United States, Canada, and to Spain, France, Germany, Sweden, and Greece in Europe, risking their lives by crossing borders and living in fear of deportation in the United States. Some went as far away as Australia. By the late 1980s, it was estimated that close to 1 million Salvadorans had left the country—about 20 percent of the total population.[4]

By the end of 1980, Ronald Reagan became the president of the United States and started to infuse massive amounts of military and economic aid to the Salvadoran government, which in turn escalated the conflict to unprecedented levels of violence. In a couple of years, the military aid given by the Reagan administration to the Salvadoran government more than tripled to amounts of more than $300 million per year. By 1982, many of the opposition groups joined the revolutionary organizations after they had exhausted all the possibilities to bring changes to the social and political systems through peaceful methods. As the opposition leadership became victims of political assassinations and disappearances at the hands of the death squads, the revolutionary organizations became more sophisticated in their organizing efforts and created the FMLN, an umbrella organization that included the most important military organizations of the Left. The FMLN began a military campaign against the military forces and repressive government organizations.

The Reagan Administration supported the government of José Napoleón Duarte as an alternative to the revolutionary movements and also attempted to get the right-wing conservative opposition under control. Duarte, a civilian, had no real control over the armed forces, but the army needed him as the president to continue receiving the military aid that kept the war going. The armed forces and the right wing were actually in control of the war efforts, as they refused to agree to a negotiated solution to the conflict. In addition, the military escalated the war effort against the FMLN during this time, a situation that clearly demonstrated that Duarte was not in control of the war strategies and social policies.

During the early 1980s, the FMLN had gained the momentum in the war, but by 1985, the military gained ground as they began to use the training, funding, and equipment provided by the United States. The military aid to the government came at a time in which the military was beginning to lose the war to the guerrillas, and the aid helped to change the balance of power in the war. The massive amounts of military aid helped the armed forces maintain a low-intensity conflict at a stalemate for almost a decade.

By 1988, the war was not just being fought in the countryside. By that time the FMLN had developed the capabilities to also run an effective urban warfare and had deployed a large percentage of their fighting force in underground activities in San Salvador and other large cities. More than 70,000 Salvadorans had died by then in the military campaigns or through government repression. The FMLN had modified its military strategy because of heavy casualties in the open war in rural areas and were trying to prepare the ground for a major offensive.

In March 1989, the ARENA party candidate Alfredo Cristiani, a powerful member of the Salvadoran upper class, was elected President, and, unlike his predecessor, he took a hard line with the FMLN groups supporting a military solution rather than a negotiated settlement to the conflict. In November 1989, the FMLN launched a major military offensive on San Salvador, after peace negotiations broke down, resulting in the deaths or injury of around 2,000 people. The military offensive against the government was not completely successful, as the FMLN was not able to take over the major cities. The psychological effect of the offensive was very important because for the first time the war was brought into the upper-class neighborhoods of the capital, and its inhabitants were terrified by the impact of the offensive. The military in return began an indiscriminate aerial bombing of working-class neighborhoods, and large numbers of civilians were killed and wounded.

In March 1991, elections resulted in the ARENA party winning 39 seats, followed by the Christian Democrats with 26. In April 1991, the outgoing members in the Legislative Assembly agreed on a set of reforms that would give more civilian control over the armed forces, create a civilian police force separate from the Army, remove judicial control from the ruling party, and improve the electoral process. With the mediation of the United Nations, President Cristiani and the FMLN signed a peace agreement that ended 12 years of civil war that had killed approximately 80,000 persons, displaced a million people inside the country, forced an additional million people to leave the country to escape the war, and caused material losses of more than $1 billion. As part of the peace agreements, a timetable was drafted for the gradual demobilization of the FMLN army; the disbandment of the National Guard and Treasury Police organizations, the reduction of the armed forces; as well as political and economic reforms that would include FMLN members.

On December 14, 1992 the demobilization of FMLN and government troops was finally complete with a ceremony the following day in San Salvador, marking the end of the civil war. The election of U.S. President Bill Clinton in 1992 brought in new policymakers with little interest in continuing the failed Reagan/Bush Salvadoran policy. Military aid to El Salvador was sharply reduced, and there was a greater insistence that the Salvadoran government comply with the 1992 Peace Accords.

In March 1993, a United Nations Truth Commission report was published, and it documented the atrocities of the 12-year civil war and found that many senior army officers were responsible for the murder of thousands of civilians. The Commission's report also urged that the officers be dismissed; be banned from public office for 10 years; and prohibited from ever gaining military or security responsibilities. Soon thereafter, the Legislative Assembly passed an amnesty law that exonerated all individuals who had committed crimes and human rights abuses during the war. The United Nations Secretary General announced that the Salvadoran government had not complied with the Peace Agreements, while the U.S. government withheld further military aid until the purge of military officers had been completed. By the end of 1993, the Salvadoran army and the police forces underwent a process of reorganization, the U.S.-trained special battalions were disbanded, the National Civilian Police was created, the FMLN turned in their weapons to the UN Peace Forces, and former combatants began to be trained for new occupations in an attempt to restructure the armed forces and the FMLN.

At this time, the United States and the European Community began to give extensive economic aid to smooth out the transition to peace and helped create numerous civilian organizations to help develop the war-ravaged communities in the countryside.

The long-term effects of the 12-year war are not always visible. Wars affect people in various ways and the war in El Salvador was no exception. During the late 1970s, the government forces only silenced selected religious, student, and labor leaders by means of torture and murder. The strategy of the war changed in the early 1980s, from selective repression to a general conflict that involved the entire population. Besides the destruction of individual lives, the other long-term effect was the erosion of the social fabric, exemplified by the breakdown of trust, security, and solidarity. The war left more than 80,000 people dead and more than 9,000 disappeared, most of whom were noncombatants killed by military missions carried out by the Salvadoran army and its paramilitary forces trained and financed by the United States. The arbitrary detention or abduction, followed by the disappearance, of the victim became a common practice of the security forces in El Salvador and Guatemala under the Doctrine of National Security. In

Central American mothers of the disappeared looking for their loved ones represented in a mural at Balmy Alley in San Francisco, CA. Photo by Carlos Texca.

El Salvador, this tactic took on a distinct dimension: the objective was to eliminate the "subversive" and to instill terror in his/her family and neighbors with the use of irregular forces, such as death squads. The uncertainty about who would be the next victim served to give the general impression of absolute control and impunity.

SALVADORAN SOCIETY AFTER THE PEACE ACCORDS

The United Nations sponsored the Truth Commission Report, which was released in March 1993. The report called on the Salvadoran government to investigate the origins, financial support, and make-up of the death squads that tortured, kidnapped, and murdered tens of thousands of people in the late 1970s and 1980s. The Alfredo Cristiani government never carried out this recommendation.

In late 1993, a series of assassinations of high-level FMLN members raised fears that death squads were making resurgence. Intense pressure from the United Nations and foreign governments forced President Cristiani to agree to the creation of a commission to investigate those high profile murders.

Negotiations between the UN and the Salvadoran government resulted in the creation of an investigative commission known as the "Grupo Conjunto." They determined the existence of two distinct organizational structures that engaged in or had the potential to commit politically motivated crimes. In urban areas, these types of activities are integrated into the overall phenomenon of organized crime that is dedicated to drug and arms trafficking, extortion, kidnapping, car theft, and robbery. These groups have ample organization, financial, and logistical capacity and involve former and current members of the security forces. Their members provide a pool for the contracting of hired assassins for political motives.

In rural zones, especially in the eastern part of the county, the report describes a "regionalization" of traditional death squads that were directed by local political and economic powers. There is evidence that former death squad members, members of the armed forces, and local government functionaries of the ARENA party controlled illegally armed groups that were used to assassinate and threaten their perceived enemies. These groups also engaged in intimidation of the population to prevent them from joining organizations or supporting development projects seen as contrary to the interests of their patrons and thus could maintain a climate of fear and insecurity. These groups support themselves through criminal activities or receive financial backing of local businessmen interested in maintaining their economic power.

CULTURE

The largest segment of the Salvadoran population is made up of mestizos—the racial and ethnic mixture of Spanish and Indian ancestry. A small segment of the population still identifies itself as Indian, and there are also a significant number of people who are of European, Middle Eastern or Asian background. Therefore, the Salvadoran cultural traditions are strongly influenced by a long history of colonialism and the social and economic control of the urban elites over the rural sector of society. It can be said that Salvadoran culture has a strong mixture of values and traditions that have their origins in the pre-Hispanic indigenous cultures of the region as well as the heritage brought to Central America by the Spanish colonizers. Salvadoran Spanish is a combination of Nahuat—the Indian language spoken in the region before the arrival of the Spanish conquerors and settlers—and the Spanish linguistic forms used during the colonial period in Central America.

Salvadoran culture is filled with images of the Indian past and the Spanish colonial heritage. There are many folktales and supernatural characters such as "la Siguanaba," a woman who possesses the spirits of unfaithful men. Her son, known as "el Cipitío," is a trickster spirit that woos young girls for their love and affection. Numerous other characters that play an important part of Salvadoran traditions and have survived throughout the centuries accompany these supernatural spirits. Some of them are of Indian origin while the Spanish brought others to the region and incorporated them into the Salvadoran cultural experience.

Since the 1970s, an influx of new cultural values and traditions originating in the United States have been introduced to the Central American region by radio and television as well as by Salvadoran immigrants who have relocated in the United States. Some of these new cultural forms may be seen in dress styles and language forms from the English language introduced in El Salvador via television, films, music, material culture, and advertising.

Salvadoran society and culture have experienced radical changes since the 1950s as a direct result of internal migrations. Large numbers of people left the rural sector and resettled in the greater San Salvador metropolitan area while seeking employment in the assembly line factories that were established around the capital city in the late 1950s and early 1960s. Many Salvadorans became urbanized and adopted the new values introduced through the mass media to the capital and the larger cities. But these new urban residents also kept many of their rural cultural traditions and values while living in the cities.

Salvadoran culture and society tends to promote a sense of strong family values and support for the family and children, but there is also the phenomenon of the "Casa Chica," or an extended family experience in which a man may have more than one household where he supports more than one woman and their children. This situation has not been studied in depth, but Salvadoran sociologists believe that it is promoted by migration, a high-density population, and the history of *machismo* that continues to exist since the colonial period. Salvadoran culture promotes patriarchal values and attitudes, and there are well-demarcated gender roles, as boys and men are expected to follow set patterns of behavior that demonstrate strong male characteristics such as a strong work ethic, support and protection for the families and children, as well as a permissive attitude toward relations with women. Men are expected to be the breadwinners and are expected to be the heads of the household, as Salvadoran men are expected to follow well-defined roles of what it is to be a man—a hard working man who is allowed to have open relations with many women and may resort to aggressive and violent behavior to protect what is his.

On the other hand, girls and women are taught to be submissive to men and must be dedicated to their children, their husband, and their home. Women are expected to be faithful and dependent on their husbands and to accept the rule of the man in the house. Salvadoran women are often prohibited from having close relations with other men besides the husband or her brothers. Young girls are sheltered and kept protected at home until they are of suitable age for marriage, and that can happen at any point after age 18 in urban centers and earlier in the rural areas. A woman is expected to find a husband before she reaches age 30; otherwise, she will be expected to have more problems in finding one at an older age. A woman is also expected to have children right after getting married, and in rural communities birth control is rarely practiced because of their Catholic views, and the husbands fears that if a woman practices birth control, then she will have more opportunities to cheat and have promiscuous relations with other men.

These cultural practices related to gender roles may be observed across social class lines and are present in urban as well as rural communities. In the past decade, some of these practices are slowly changing in the capital but continue to exist in rural communities. This is a cultural element that has also been carried by Salvadoran immigrants to their newly established communities and cultural settings in the United States.

WORLD VIEW AND RELIGION

The official religion of El Salvador is the Roman Catholic faith, and approximately 83 percent of the Salvadoran people are practicing Catholics.

It is important to note though, that the Catholic religion that is practiced in El Salvador and the rest of Central America and Mexico is strongly influenced by the ancient indigenous Mesoamerican religious traditions. What is actually practiced in Central America is a mixture of religious beliefs coming from the ancient indigenous religious practices with the Catholic traditions and practices of the sixteenth century. As the centuries passed, this form of religious expression only slightly changed. On other hand, Protestant groups have been very active throughout the country for the past 50 years. It is estimated that there are approximately 1 million Protestant evangelicals in El Salvador at this time.

Religion has been the central force in the cultures and civilizations that have existed in Central America throughout the centuries. The importance of religion and its predominance in society can be traced to pre-Hispanic times. When the Catholic missionaries imposed Catholicism on the indigenous population, the native religion, conception of the world, and importance of the supernatural world did not disappear. Ancient ritual and belief took a covert role in the religious practice of the Central American people, and the resulting phenomenon was the adaptation of Catholicism into the native religion throughout the entire cultural region of Mexico and Central America.

In El Salvador, as in most regions of Latin America, Catholicism has become the dominant factor in the contemporary belief systems of the population. An important factor for this cultural change was the systematic persecution of those who practiced the ancient indigenous religions by the Office of the Holy Inquisition created by the Catholic Church in Europe and brought to the Americas by the Spanish missionaries. In the rural areas and provinces, the animistic view of the world and the supernatural realm dominate the religious spectrum. This animistic view expresses the belief that everything that is naturally created in the universe has a spirit or soul and must be respected as a living entity. It includes all humans, Mother Earth, animals, rocks, natural formations, rivers, lakes, mountains, the sun, the moon, the planets, the stars, and all forms in the creation of the cosmos. It is common belief that if one eats the flesh of an animal, its attributes will be passed on to the person by means of sympathetic magic. These ideas are similar to those in the ancient Mesoamerican religion. Among the indigenous communities, the role of the native traditional religion still has strong social control over the lifestyle of the population, especially among the elder generations. In San Salvador, the Catholic beliefs dominate the religious life of the urbanized people. But individuals that migrated from the rural areas to the cities have brought with them the native religious ideology that is widely practiced in the countryside, thus creating a blended religious practice among the urban working class.

The contemporary "Catholic" worldview is based on the conception that humanity is surrounded by the environment *(ambiente)*, which is controlled by God. Life is a constant interaction between the three elements, air, fire, and water, and the dualistic forces of nature. Humans can manipulate the environment only if God permits it. So in turn, humanity has to be on good terms and have a close and dedicated relationship with God and the Catholic saints to use the environment for survival. The environment is manipulated to create a balance in the dualistic forces of nature, to bring well-being and good fortune to humanity.

Humanity must follow the religious norms and values. Attendance to rituals and ceremonies is strictly required by the religion. Whenever favors are petitioned to God, a person has to give offerings beforehand in order for the petition to be considered by the divinities. The offerings are usually in the form of candles, flowers, songs, prayer, tobacco, incense burnings, food, or liquor. On certain occasions a feast or a prayer ceremony is offered to receive the desired benefits from the divine forces.

These religious views also follow the ancient indigenous belief in the concept of duality. All forms of creation, including the divinity, have a dualistic nature. They can be creative and give all types of blessings; or they can be destructive and cause many types of harm to humans or the environment. If a person does not follow the rules of religious tradition, it is believed that God can turn the destructive aspects of the environment against the individual as a form of punishment. The types of punishment usually take the form of evil winds, hurricanes, drought, flood, thunder, lightning, loss of agricultural crops, or bodily harm. It is popularly believed that God sends these punishments when a person has gravely sinned.

The Catholic saints play an important role in the life of the Salvadoran people. The saints are envisioned to live in an environment like an earthly paradise. They have lived their life as humans and are thought to behave as such. They eat, sleep, feel, laugh, suffer and cry in the same manner that humans do. Humans must be on good terms with the Catholic saints and must make offerings of candles, prayer, flowers, and other items to them, because the saints act as intermediaries between God and humanity. They are the only beings who can deal directly with God about worldly affairs, as it is commonly believed that humans cannot communicate directly with God.

The Catholic saints have a well-defined hierarchy among themselves. Some are devoted to the protection of specific problems, afflictions, or illnesses. Some are closer to God than others, while others are associated with the attributes of ancient Mesoamerican deities or with the Christian Devil himself. Some examples of the saints and their attributes are as follows: St. Christopher is the patron saint of travelers and drivers. His popularity has persisted throughout Central America even though he was removed from the ranks of sainthood by the Catholic church in the late 1960s (because of a lack of historical documentation that he ever existed). St. Lucy is the protector of individuals who suffer from eye ailments. She is popularly represented with her eyes on a silver platter that she holds in her hand. San Diego is the protector of the poor. San Isidro Labrador is the protector of the farmers and plantations and is often associated with the ancient agricultural gods of Mesoamerica. The Virgin of El Carmen is the protector in the hour of death. San Simon is thought to be one of the Lords of the Underworld by the Indian people, whereas the non-Indian people *(ladinos)* see him as the Devil.

In El Salvador, most people are dedicated and devoted to their favorite protector saints, practicing rituals that require prayer, candles, incense, and much attention. All towns and cities have a patron saint, and there are yearly celebrations and festivities in honor of the patron saint's day. Many towns and cities are also named after the patron saint; such is the case of the country of El Salvador named after the Savior of the world, also Santa Ana, San Miguel, and many more. During the festivities dedicated to the patron saint, all the promises and penance offered to the saint are performed in gratitude for all the favors granted or requested. These favors can be such as a good crop of corn, good weather, good health, etc.

It is popularly believed that a person cannot solve his/her problems without the help of God and the mediation of the Catholic saints. For a person to receive the help of a saint, offerings of money, flowers, liquor, food, candles, tobacco, and many other ritual objects are placed at the home or at the church altar. All of the offerings must be given in advance, before requesting any favors, in order to maintain harmony and good standing with the saints. This practice of giving offerings before an invocation was widely practiced in ancient Mesoamerica; at present, the Catholic saints have taken the role of the ancient deities. When the saints do not respond to the prayers and petitions, offerings, and ritual performances, an individual has the option of punishing the saints. The image of the saint is wrapped and put away in a dark place, or the image is tied with a red ribbon that will not allow its spirit to go anywhere, or the image is placed upside down until the petition is granted and favorable results occur.

The conception of the universe among rural people of El Salvador is of an animistic nature. The environment or *ambiente* is everything that surrounds humankind, everything that can be perceived and that can affect humans. Included in this definition of the environment are the supernatural forces, evil spirits, and dark forces of the devil. The supernatural realm tries to dominate humanity, which is why people must learn how to interact with the supernatural in the same manner that they have to learn to deal with everything else in their surroundings.

According to sixteenth-century Catholic beliefs, humans are born in sin. Only the will of God and living a good life according to the traditions and values will bring health and fortune to an individual. Suffering is considered to be part of human nature and death is associated as a punishment for a person's sins. An individual who does not follow the traditions, values, morals, and taboos of the community will be an outcast among the rest of the members and will continuously be threatened by witchcraft, sorcery, and feelings of envy.

TRADITIONAL MEDICINE–PHILOSOPHY AND PRACTICE

Traditional beliefs in Central America hold that sometimes God selects an individual to be sick. The illness is sent as a lesson for the religious person to keep a good life and not to go astray. The individual must play the same role that Christ played on the cross. He/she must accept the will of God. Many of these especially selected individuals also acquire healing powers after recovery, which they must pay back to the saints by working as healers. Most people see illness as part of the will of God and the Catholic saints. These ideas conflict with the basic concepts of Western medicine. Medical doctors and specialists in the hospitals and health clinics of El Salvador do not agree with the popular ideas about supernatural causes of disease, which, according to the population, can only be treated by a spiritual healer (curandero).

A high percentage of the rural population and also a significant number of urban residents seek the services of a curandero before going to a health clinic or a medical doctor. They hesitate to get the services of a medical doctor because of beliefs that forced sterilization and population control are commonly practiced at government medical facilities. Curanderos have a great body of knowledge about the medical uses of native plants, minerals, and animals in their environment. The curandero uses all these materials to create remedies for the most common afflictions and illnesses that affect the population. Curanderos also have knowledge of magical secrets and magical prayers that will aid in the healing of supernatural illnesses.

When a campesino has a minor ailment, he seeks advice from a relative or a friend to help in the diagnosis of the ailment and to prescribe the proper remedy. The knowledge of the traditional methods of healing, the native use of plants and substances of animal or mineral origin for curing, and the belief in the supernatural are widespread throughout the rural areas and in the urban neighborhoods *(barrios)*. Most people in the rural areas know which plants to use for a minor ailment, especially those that are of natural origins.

When the affliction is a major illness, then the patient seeks the help of an *entendido* or "one who knows." This ritual specialist can be a *curandero*, sorcerer, massager, bonesetter, herbalist, or a spiritualist. The remedies used in the traditional methods of healing by these specialists fall in different categories depending on the origin of the illness and the religious convictions and cultural patterns of the individual. The following is a description of the categories of remedies:

1. The extensive knowledge about the uses of native plants and minerals handed down through generations. These remedies are of pre-Hispanic and European origin. With the introduction of European pharmacopoeia, the old systems adopted new remedies. The native remedies are prepared from flowers, leaves, roots, branches, barks, bulbs, seeds, nuts, resins, animal and vegetable fats, waxes, fruits, minerals, etc.

2. With the introduction of modern European and U.S. medical practices, the use of medicines and remedies based on Euro-centric pharmacopoeia has become very popular among the urban people. They are less popular in the rural areas. These remedies are in the form of pills, capsules, injections, ointments, balms, syrups, and other pharmaceutical products. Most pharmaceutical drugs are sold over the counter without a prescription written by a medical doctor. Many of the drugs that are presently in the market are prohibited or controlled in the United States and Europe where they are manufactured.

3. Another category of traditional remedies are those that are used for the treatment of supernatural illnesses caused by witchcraft, strong vision, ghosts, the Catholic saints, the planets, or any other natural or supernatural phenomena. The remedies used are selected according to the origin of the illness. The remedies can be of various types; they could be Catholic prayers or secret prayers to the Devil or supernatural spirits, exorcisms, baths, incense burnings, magic words and phrases, chants, amulets, charms, spells, talismans, and other objects used in specific rituals and ceremonies. All of the supernatural illnesses have to be attended by an *entendido* or specialist, but there are also everyday people who have the power and knowledge to cure some diseases, especially those that affect young children and infants. Some of these diseases are *mal ojo* (evil eye), fallen fontanel, and *susto* (magical fright).

In rural El Salvador, the beliefs about the supernatural realm are very common among the population as they play a major role in their belief system. The supernatural realm is always present as a parallel reality, and a person must know how to act in difficult situations when there are encounters with evil supernatural forces, otherwise there is the possibility of running the risk of falling ill or even death. Salvadorans believe that supernatural forces or spirits are the owners of natural phenomena and the environment. A large number of people actually believe that in nearby rivers, caves, hills, mountains, ravines, lakes, etc., live spirits that own these aspects of the environment. If a person desires to enter the domain of the supernatural spirits, then offerings must be given and permission must be requested in order to enter safely. This permission is requested through prayers and invocations. If hunting, fishing, or cutting of trees in their territories is desired, then offerings must be given in the form of food, candles, liquor, incense, flowers, tobacco, and prayer. If these offerings are not given to the spirits, then the trespasser runs the risk of being afflicted by a supernatural illness sent by the spirit owners of the natural resources.

Supernatural illnesses affect mainly young children and infants, especially if the child has not been baptized or does not carry or wear any protective amulets and talismans. Men and women are also affected by supernatural illnesses especially if they engage in behavior that goes against the rules of the society. They can also be affected if they are weak individuals and have a weak soul. Older people are seldom affected by the supernatural illnesses, as it is commonly believed that an older person has a strong spirit.

If a person suffers from hypertension and is constantly in a state of fear of witchcraft and sorcery, the anguish and anxiety can bring through its own bad suggestion a state of *susto* or magical fright. The symptoms of the patient are extreme anguish and fear, fast and strong breathing, itching of the face, palpitations of the heart, and cramps. It is commonly accepted that when a person is affected by *susto* because the soul is weak, it escapes the body of the patient, leaving him in a state of anxiety, depression, and even coma. In traditional Latin American societies, it is popularly accepted that soul loss is strongly related to *susto*. Soul loss can also take place by means of witchcraft and sorcery.

Most of these religious beliefs and medical practices are brought by Central American and Salvadoran immigrants to Salvadoran communities in the United States, therefore, as they go on with their daily lives in this country, they continue to maintain a strong belief system that is incompatible with the U.S. views on religion and health. Many serious conflicts arise from the belief conflicts, and immigrants and their children, after a long period of residence in the United States, begin to adopt new ways of looking at religion and healing.

NOTES

1. Jorge Arias Gomez, *Farabundo Marti* (San Salvador, El Salvador: Editorial Universitaria Centroamericana, 1972.) Thomas Anderson. *El Salvador 1932.* Editorial Universitaria Centroamericana (EDUCA) 1976.

2. Amnesty International, "Extrajudicial Executions in El Salvador: Report of an Amnesty International Mission to Examine Post-mortem and Investigative Procedures" (Amnesty International, 1984).

3. Lauren Gilbert. *El Salvador's Death Squads: New Evidence from U.S. Documents.* (Washington, D.C.: Center for International Policy, March 1994).

4. Carlos B. Cordova and Felix S. Kury, "Central American Mental Health Intervention Strategies." In *Latino Mental Health Perspectives in the United States,* ed. Alberto Lopez (Bethesda, MD: National Institute of Mental Health, Fall 1999).

PART II

COMING TO THE UNITED STATES AND STATUS

2

U.S. Immigration Laws for Salvadorans and Status

SALVADORAN IMMIGRANTS AND U.S. IMMIGRATION LAWS 1980–2004

Since the late 1970s legal immigration from Latin American countries accounted for about 40 percent of the total number of immigrants arriving in the United States. According to the 1980 Census, Mexicans have been ranking at the top of the Latin American immigration figures, with Central American countries coming next for contributing significant Latin American migrations to the United States. Immigration scholars have stated that the world economic crisis and the political instability that have been facing Latin America have increased the numbers of undocumented immigrants from the region to the United States. Approximately 80 percent of all undocumented immigrants in the United States are of Mexican origin, and since the 1980s there has been a significant increase in the numbers of new undocumented immigrants arriving in the United States from the Central American region.

Since 1979, population movements out of El Salvador have increased as a direct result of the crisis that was generated by the political and military conflicts in that Central American country. Many communities in areas of military conflict were evacuated and forcefully moved by the Salvadoran armed forces. The inhabitants of these communities were either relocated in refugee camps throughout El Salvador, fled to other Central American countries where they lived in extreme poverty in refugee camps, or migrated to Canada, the United States, or Europe as undocumented immigrants. Estimates state that more than 500,000 refugees were found in various camps inside El Salvador during the 1980s and early 1990s. More than 300,000 people were found living in refugee camps in the Central American region and anywhere from 300,000 to 500,000 undocumented Salvadorans sought refuge in the United States.[1]

Based on these figures, more than 20 percent of the Salvadoran population is believed to be presently residing outside El Salvador. Estimates of the Salvadoran population throughout the United States range from 708,741 to 1,117,959 people.

To fully understand the dynamics of the migration processes, careful considerations must be given to the experiences of the process of migration. Migration may be defined as a relative permanent moving away of a group of people from their traditional place of residence. They are called migrants, as they have relocated from one geographical location to another, their decisions to migrate were either voluntary or involuntary, and in just about all cases the migrants experience a kind of culture shock upon their arrival in the new host society.

When the existing social conditions in the country of origin fail to satisfy individual needs, members of the community may consider the options of moving away to new places to overcome their deprivation. Furthermore, if the conditions that led to the migration continue to exist after their relocation in a new social environment, and if the migrants continue to attach a high value to their expectations and desired ends, then the adjustment difficulties might force the migrants to experience a second migration to another more hospitable environment, or a return migration to their original home can be expected.

The previous criteria are applicable to the study of economic migrants, who are usually motivated to leave their country of origin as described in the push-pull theories. If economic migrants are dissatisfied in the host country, they have the option of returning to the country of origin or moving on to a new social environment where they can experience better economic and social opportunities. In the case of political or involuntary migrations, there are extreme difficulties in demonstrating the political or economic nature of the migration process.

In many cases, people who have been thought to be political refugees have been found to be motivated to migrate out of their countries because of economic rather than political reasons. On the other hand, migrations believed to be economically motivated may in reality have political origins. The political decisions of national states have frequent and major consequences for the socioeconomic context in which individual decisions are made. Political processes may turn out to induce migration, directly or indirectly, as they constrain the economic opportunities available to the general population or particular segments of it.

Besides the changing socioeconomic realities experienced by immigrants in the United States, there is hardly any other policy context that has affected so thoroughly the life of most Salvadoran immigrants living in the United States, than that of immigration. The changing U.S. immigration policies since the 1980s have directly affected the vast majority of this community. From those who live as undocumented immigrants, to those who go through the process of becoming naturalized U.S. citizens, the immigration policy arenas represent a common area of difficulties among Salvadorans.

REFUGEE STATUS AND POLITICAL ASYLUM

Before 1980, the immigration law did not have a formal definition of refugee, although there was a provision that allowed for the admission of up to 17,400 persons fleeing from persecution in a communist or communist dominated country or within the general area of the Middle East. However, since the enactment of the 1980 Refugee Act, there are now distinct classifications for refugee and political asylum applicants. Through this Act, a refugee is defined in accordance with the 1951 United Nations Convention definition as a person who, having demonstrated a well-founded fear of persecution because of race, religion, nationality, or membership in a particular social or political organization, is outside the country of his/her nationality, and is unable or unwilling to receive the protection of that country. It is important to note that for an individual to qualify as a refugee, that person must be residing outside the United States territory. A person applying for political asylum must meet the same criteria as a refugee; the only difference in the process is the actual location of the individual at the time of the application. The political asylum applicant must be already in the United States or applying for admission at a port of entry, while the refugee applicant must be located outside the United States.

The criteria for accepting individuals as refugees are designated by the President of the United States in consultation with Congress and must be of special humanitarian concern to the United States. The Immigration Act allows the President to designate certain countries where the refugee applications may be processed within their own homelands. Factors considered are the plight of the refugees, human rights violations in the country of origin, and family, historical, cultural, or religious ties in the United States. The likelihood of finding sanctuary elsewhere, as well as previous contacts with the U.S. government, must be taken into consideration before granting refugee status. After the refugee has been admitted to the United States, he/she may be granted permanent resident status after one year of residence.[2]

Additionally, the Refugee Act provides financial and program assistance to refugees to help in resettlement. This type of aid is exemplified by the aid given to recent refugees from southeast Asia since 1975. Included in the Act is a new designation of political asylum for those people who are deemed refugees and who are in the United States or who are applying for admission at a land border or port of entry. Asylum is a discretionary act exercised by the Attorney General that allows the refugee to remain in the United States as opposed to being deported. It is not the equivalent of refugee status, as refugees may have their status changed to permanent resident one year after their entry into the United States. Persons granted political asylum may not be able to change their immigration status as easily, even though the law stipulates that they can become permanent residents after living one year in the United States.

On the surface, the 1980 Act is a nondiscriminatory law that determines political asylum on the basis of the origin of the refugee. However, countries from which refugees seem to have serious difficulties in obtaining political asylum often have close political ties to the United States. Because the U.S. government perceives undocumented Salvadorans as economic immigrants, it denies their claims of persecution. In order to be granted political asylum, refugees must prove they are legitimate refugees. According to the 1980 Act, the burden of proof rested with the refugee, who must show a well-founded fear of persecution. But the Supreme Court established that the refugee must show a clear probability of persecution to avoid deportation.

The establishment of clear probability required extensive documentation. The amount of documentation necessary depended on the U.S. Department of State perceptions of the country's human rights practices, especially in countries receiving U.S. governmental aid. Later in 1987, in *Cardoza-Fonseca v. Immigration and Naturalization Service* (INS), the Supreme Court held that a well-founded fear of persecution is a reasonable fear, and that the clear probability of persecution was not a necessary test. The Board of Immigration Appeals in the matter of Mogharrabi (1987) adopted the reasonable fear test. An immigrant applying for asylum would have to prove reasonable fear if the individual believed that a persecutor sought to punish him/her. The individual had to prove that the persecutor could become aware of his/her belief. In addition, the individual would have to prove that the persecutor has the means and inclination to punish the individual. Fear is considered subjective if the individual is actually fearful (Matter of Acosta; *Guevara-Flores v. INS*) and is considered objective if the fear is based on a clear reality or reasonable probability (Matter of Acosta; *INS v. Stevic*, 1984).

For the INS to grant refugee status or political asylum, an advisory opinion from the Bureau of Human Rights and Humanitarian Affairs of the State Department is taken into consideration in the final ruling. It was common practice for the State Department in the 1980s to issue form letters regarding Salvadoran refugees, stating that Salvadorans did not qualify as refugees as defined in the Refugee Act of 1980. In 1981, the United Nations High Commission on Refugees disagreed with this view and expressed that Salvadorans in the United States were prima facie refugees and should have not been deported or forced to return to El Salvador. They requested that the U.S. government give temporary refuge to the Salvadorans by granting them extended voluntary departure. See Table 2.1 for the actual numbers of political asylum application filed by Salvadorans between 1987 and 2001.

Table 2.1
Refugee and Asylum Application Filed by Salvadorans with the INS, 1987–2001

Year	Asylum Applicants	Asylum Cases Reopened	Asylum Granted	Refugee Arrivals	Asylees and Refugees Granted Residency
1987	2,684	N/A	39	74	172
1988	27,048	N/A	149	60	170
1989	29,680	N/A	443	74	198
1990	22,271	N/A	260	136	245
1991	10,244	N/A	185	110	1249
1992	6,781	N/A	110	259	743
1993	14,616	N/A	74	1,006	811
1994	18,600	N/A	185	N/A	275
1995	75,860	N/A	234	0	283
1996	65,588	N/A	198	0	262
1997	8,156	3,450	182	0	128
1998	3,847	2,498	388	0	129
1999	2,008	1,046	296	0	47
2000	1,006	863	146	0	76
2001	725	746	158	0	195
2002	274	597	75	0	187

Source: Statistical Yearbooks of the INS 1987–2002.

In 1984, the American Civil Liberties Union also requested that the Reagan Administration grant Extended Voluntary Departure (EVD) to Salvadorans. This was request was based on the fact that EVD had been used by the U.S. government in the past and had allowed citizens of other countries that were experiencing dangerous conditions to remain in the United States temporarily. It had also allowed them to receive work permits while living in the United States. Extended Voluntary Departure is granted at the discretion of the U.S. Attorney General, upon the recommendation of the Secretary of State, and the extended voluntary departure status is revoked once the hostilities and endangerment have ended in the alien's home country and safety has been restored. Ethiopians, Poles, Lebanese, Ugandans, and Afghanis have enjoyed EVD status.

The U.S. government denied political asylum or extended voluntary departure to Salvadorans because it reasoned that Salvadorans had left the Central American region merely due to fears of being caught in the violence generated by the political struggles between the Right and the Left. In reality, there is evidence that directly implicated the Salvadoran government armed forces with the right-wing political violence that was a major cause of civilian deaths in that country. Evidence has been presented by human rights organizations and U.S. Congressional and Labor investigations such as the National Labor Committee that stated that virtually all the political prisoners they had spoken to had been tortured. There were victims of beatings, electric shock, suffocation, and sleep deprivation. The torture inevitably came at the hands of internal security forces, often in private residences.

The American Civil Liberties Union analyzed the cases of 8,500 Salvadoran deportees between 1981–1983 and found conclusive evidence in 112 cases of abductions, torture, disappearances, murder, and other acts of political violence. The record was sparse because of the extreme difficulty of monitoring persons deported, and information is difficult to obtain in El Salvador.[3] It was evident that asylum criteria were arbitrarily implemented by the U.S. government, as exemplified by the Mariel Cuban exodus in 1980, during which approximately 125,000 Cubans were granted political asylum by the United States. Studies have indicated that a significant number of Cuban refugees did not leave the island because they were subjected to political persecution but rather because of the lack of economic opportunities available to them.

Large numbers of undocumented Salvadorans living in the United States have stated that they relocated in this country because of political rather than economic reasons. These assertions may be documented by the fact that before the civil war, between 1970 and 1980, the Salvadoran political asylum applications were almost nonexistent. Only 45 Salvadorans who had applied for political asylum were granted permanent resident status. On the other hand, lawful permanent residence status was granted to 1,383 Salvadorans in the 1980s and 4,073 Salvadorans in the 1990s who applied for either political asylum or refugee status in the United States. However, until recently only 3 percent of all applicants were granted political asylum. In 1984, the INS rejected 13,045 Salvadoran petitions for political asylum and granted only 328; on the other hand, 3,890 Salvadorans were deported. According to INS official sources, 273,372 Salvadorans applied for political asylum between 1987 and 1996, and only 1,877 Salvadorans were granted asylum.

In July 1997, the Clinton administration took a step forward in helping the case of Salvadoran applicants that had been denied political asylum. Attorney General Janet Reno mandated to reopen the political asylum cases that had been denied and that new laws would not be applied to pending cases because they would have harsh effects on them. The Illegal Immigration Reform and Immigrant Responsibility Act of 1996 (IIRIRA) severely restricts suspension of deportation, which is often the remedy available to deportable aliens who have lived in the United States for considerably long periods of time. Under the old law, suspension could be granted, at the discretion of the immigration judge, to an alien who has been living in the United States for seven years, who demonstrated good moral character, and who could prove that deportation would cause extreme hardship to the alien or to a spouse, parent, or child who is a lawful permanent resident or U.S. citizen. That would be the standard to be followed in the case of Salvadoran asylum applicants. Between 1997 and 2002, approximately 9,200 old cases were reopened and 16,016 new cases were submitted to the INS for review. During this same period of time 1,245 Salvadorans were granted political asylum.

Since 2002, the standard of "proof of persecution" is a difficult one to present for a number of reasons. The war ended in El Salvador in 1992, and the United States strongly believes that political persecution and repression ended at the time of the signing of the Peace Agreements in El Salvador and therefore continues to deny most cases. Most recently, since the INS became part of the Department of Homeland Security, the standards of proof are more difficult to prove, and the new antiterrorist laws are directly applied to aliens who are not considered to have good moral character, or who have been arrested for crimes such as driving under the influence, domestic violence, or any other felony.

The United States has traditionally allowed liberal immigration practices when dealing with political refugees from totalitarian communist countries, but not from friendly totalitarian or authoritarian noncommunist dictatorships. In cases from communist countries, asylum applicants have been granted the asylum status quickly. In the case of Salvadoran asylum applicants, the INS was slow to decide cases and has kept an extremely large backlog of pending cases. Because of the close relationship with the Salvadoran government, which benefits the economic and political interests of the United States, the U.S. State Department policy denied political asylum or extended voluntary departure to most Salvadorans who applied for that status. The policies and practices of the U.S. State Department, specifically the policies and procedures of the INS, negatively affected undocumented Salvadorans. The denial of political asylum created additional cultural and social adaptation problems for the undocumented Salvadorans, such as lack of work permits and fear of persecution from INS officers, a situation that makes the acculturation and adaptation processes a much more difficult experience. The social, economic, and political policies of a receiving society may either help to ease the normal adjustment or frustrate the resettlement of recently arrived immigrants. There is ample empirical evidence to show that hostile or inhospitable social policies and institutional practices lead to such negative consequences as unemployment or underemployment, poor housing, low educational attainment in immigrant children, antisocial behavior, and a wide variety of mental health problems.

THE UNDOCUMENTED SALVADORAN POPULATION

The term undocumented Salvadorans is used here to describe (a) persons born in El Salvador who entered the United States without an immigration visa and crossed the border without an immigration inspection, (b) individuals who entered the country with a student or tourist visa but have overstayed as their visas expired, (c) persons who lawfully entered the United States for a specified length of time but violated the terms of their temporary visa, (d) those individuals who have not changed their status to legal permanent resident, and (e) persons who have applied and received temporary protected status from deportation. The U.S. government and the mass media often use the term *illegal alien* to refer to these individuals, but the term does not have widespread acceptance in the Latino/Chicano communities of the United States, as it is often considered derogatory and insulting. Furthermore, the term illegal alien does not appear in a single section of the immigration laws. Aliens are either deportable or lawfully within the United States.

Some sectors of the U.S. society have a different perception of the term *undocumented* based on the premise that Latino and other community leaders do not agree to the use of the term illegal alien and prefer the term undocumented, which is believed to be misleading because these migrants bring a number of birth certificates, employment records, and relatives' addresses to gain entry to the United States.[4] This interpretation does not hold true in the case of undocumented Salvadorans who were reported to carry very few documents while traveling to the United States during the 1980s. Proof of being from El Salvador could have been a dangerous thing in the long journey north. If Guatemalan, Mexican, or U.S. immigration officials or police officers detained a Salvadoran national, the individual was usually deported back to El Salvador. If an individual did not carry documents, then this person may have claimed that he/she was of Mexican origin and could have been deported to or remained in Mexican territory. That would allow the person an additional opportunity to try to cross the U.S. border one more time. Moreover, these countries that Salvadorans had to cross to travel to the United States did not offer safety or sanctuary even on a temporary basis; therefore, it was unsafe to claim a Salvadoran or Guatemalan origin while being detained there.

Early 1982 INS estimates of undocumented Salvadorans in the United States were believed to be higher than 500,000. Those high figures were eventually modified as a result of the legalization process of undocumented Salvadorans under the Immigration Reform and Control Act of 1986 (IRCA), Temporary Protected Status (TPS), as well as the actual deportation of Salvadorans during that time. In 1986, it was estimated that between 4 and 12 million undocumented people were residing in the United States. By 1987, the INS estimates lowered the figure to 3.4 million. Mexico lead the undocumented population figures while El Salvador ranked at the number two position.

According to INS figures, in 1993 the estimated Salvadoran undocumented population was approximately 327,000 people, still ranking as the second largest population of undocumented immigrants in the United States. In 1996, the INS estimated the total figures of the undocumented population to be approximately 5 million people. They have also estimated that during the 1990s, the undocumented population grew by 350,000 each year. By January 2000, the INS estimated that 7 million unauthorized undocumented immigrants were residing in the United States. Mexico continued to rank at the top as the largest source of undocumented workers, and the INS estimated the Mexican undocumented population to have risen from 2 million in 1990 to 4.8 million in January 2000. In addition to Mexico, in

January 2000, six other countries had more than 100,000 undocumented immigrants living in the United States. El Salvador continued to rank second with 189,000 undocumented immigrants in the United States. The Salvadoran figures in January 2000 are lower than the 298,000 Salvadoran undocumented workers estimated in 1990 because the new figures do not include many undocumented Salvadorans who were granted TPS during the decade. In 1997 many long-term undocumented persons from El Salvador, Guatemala, Nicaragua, Cuba, and the former Soviet Union were allowed to stay and legally work in the United States under the provisions of the Nicaraguan Adjustment and Central American Relief Act (NACARA).

It is also important to note that according to INS data, the great majority of undocumented persons are found in California. The largest number of Salvadoran immigrants in the United States have relocated in California, especially in the Los Angeles–Long Beach metropolitan areas. The Los Angeles metropolitan area has the second largest population of Salvadorans in the world at this time. It would be safe to say then that the largest number of undocumented Salvadorans could be found in the southern California region.

The undocumented population estimates may be useful only for limited generalizations. Nonetheless, the undocumented and their experience in the labor market can be researched from a variety of sources employing different methodologies. Studies can be made from people apprehended by the INS, from surveys of unapprehended undocumented workers, interviews with return migrants living in their areas of origin, and data collected from legal immigrants with previous experience of working illegally in the United States.

Undocumented persons often fear the official government authorities and the possibility of deportation by the INS. Salvadorans particularly feared deportation because of the violence that has been affecting their country during the past two decades. Even though the war technically ended in 1992, the post-war violence has escalated to a level never seen during the actual fighting that took place in the 1980s. It must be noted that many Salvadorans who might be repatriated from the United States would be displaced persons upon arrival. As such they would be particularly vulnerable to random or arbitrary violence. During the 1980s, many undocumented persons entered the United States because of persecution by the Salvadoran government on account of political activities. Others left El Salvador because of the social chaos, disorder, and lack of personal safety created by the war conditions.

The U.S. Department of State firmly maintained that undocumented persons come to this country because of economic reasons, wanting to improve their socioeconomic status. The official government position is in agreement with the push-pull theories of economic migrations. The country of origin where the economic system is weak and unstable creates the push. The pull effect is generated by the economic stability experienced by the host country, in this case the United States, attracting people because of a strong economic foundation and low unemployment rates.

Some of these Salvadoran undocumented persons entered the U.S. territory because of persecution that they experienced from the Salvadoran government on account of political memberships or activities. Others left El Salvador because of the social chaos, disorder, and lack of personal safety created by the war conditions. Before 1979, the push-pull theory could have been applicable to the migration patterns of both documented and undocumented Salvadorans coming to this country. The controversy arises with the post-1979 migration patterns. In an analysis of the sociopolitical reality of El Salvador, the U.S. foreign policy for the region and INS practices, there is evidence of conflicts in the implementation of policies and practices in the domestic and foreign affairs of the United States government. There are a wide range of politically influenced factors that generated the migration out of El Salvador. Between 1979 and 1992, the sociopolitical reality of El Salvador exploded into a state of political crisis and civil war. U.S. foreign policy clearly admitted to this fact as documented by official sources and extensive reports published throughout a wide range of national and international mass media publications. U.S. foreign policy recognized existence of the civil strife in the Central American region as it was observed in the escalating U.S. military involvement in the area and the official policy statements on the region during that time.[5]

On the other hand, when the U.S. Department of State decided domestic policies, it proposed that the Salvadoran government was not a totalitarian dictatorship that persecuted its citizens. The notion that there was a civil war was rejected by the State Department, and Salvadorans were viewed as emigrating from their country to escape the violence created by factions of the Right and the Left as well as for economic reasons. According to this position, Salvadorans were emigrating in large numbers because of the serious economic problems existing in Central America. This interpretation of U.S. policies affected the immigration policies and practices and, as a result, undocumented Salvadorans were denied political asylum in the United States. Moreover, President Reagan stated on June 20, 1983, in a press conference in Washington, D.C., that if the political crisis was not resolved, thousands of refugees were expected to come to the United States not as "boat people" but as "foot people."

THE SANCTUARY MOVEMENT, RELIGIOUS COMMUNITIES, AND SALVADORAN REFUGEES IN THE UNITED STATES

During the early 1980s approximately 250,000 Central American refugees entered the United States escaping the wars in their home countries. Most of them entered the United States illegally using "coyotes" or professional smugglers to get them safely across the border. Many people die every year trying to cross the border, especially during the hot summer months. After the deaths of 21 Salvadoran undocumented immigrants in the Arizona desert in 1980, many Americans became aware of the immigrants' struggles and their attempts to find refuge and political asylum in the United States.

Jim Corbett, a retired rancher from Tucson, Arizona, was one of the first Americans to become actively involved in helping Central American refugees find safety and refuge in the United States. His efforts in helping Central American refugees became part of a popular movement in religious communities that spread rapidly across the country. Corbett tried to work within the law to help the refugees by helping apply for political asylum, but as the INS began a campaign of arrests and deportations of Central Americans, Corbett began to challenge the federal government by helping to smuggle Central American refugees from the Mexican border into Arizona and placing them in safe homes of religious workers and lay people. The wars in El Salvador and Guatemala intensified and as more Central Americans arrived, the U.S. government did not consider them to be political refugees but rather economic migrants. They were quickly deported back to Central America unless they could prove that they had a "well-founded fear of persecution," and under the conditions of their flight and the persecutions and the repression taking place in their home countries, it was very difficult to prove. In addition, the U.S. government did not consider Salvadorans and Guatemalans to be political refugees, because they were fleeing countries that were considered close allies of the Unites States fighting against the communist threat affecting the region and were at the same time staunch enemies of Fidel Castro's Cuba and the Sandinistas in Nicaragua.

After two years of helping hundreds of Central Americans cross the border, Corbett brought the struggle of Central American refugees to national attention. He sought the support of the Tucson Ecumenical Council, and with the help of Rev. John Fife, the pastor of the Southside Presbyterian Council, on March 24, 1982, they publicly opened their churches and declared them a sanctuary to the newly arrived refugees. Soon after, the movement spread even more rapidly throughout the country and more than 330 churches became part of the Sanctuary Movement. The Sanctuary Movement was an effective national program for involving congregations in support of Central American refugees. The activists engaged in the movement integrated direct relief actions, public policy advocacy, and civil disobedience.

In the case of undocumented Salvadorans relocating in the southwestern United States, they were readily welcomed by numerous religious communities, as demonstrated by the high levels of support toward the sanctuary movement and the number of social work organizations that provided services for them. An underground railroad and a network of churches of various religious denominations organized across the country assisted undocumented Central American immigrants to enter the United States and offered sanctuary in their churches and in their religious communities. They provided them with housing, employment, legal services, and basic survival programs to allow them to adjust to their new life in the United States. The movement motivated parishioners to open their houses to the refugees, and churches openly debated whether to allow the churches to defy the law of the government in favor of the law of God of welcoming refugees in need.

The Sanctuary organizations would provide sanctuary—support, protection, and advocacy—to low income and indigent refugees and immigrants. They also provided free or low cost legal immigration assistance and also worked to empower and encourage the civic participation of the refugee and immigrant population and to educate local religious communities and the wider public about circumstances that cause refugees to flee their homelands. In their education programs, they also involved the refugees and immigrants in telling their own personal testimonials as the means to educate the local communities, but, must importantly, the testimonials helped the refugees to cope with the trauma and stresses experienced in their homeland.

At the beginning, the movement had little impact on the INS because the number of people smuggled into the United States was relatively small as compared with the number of deportation cases handled by the INS. Until the end of 1984, the INS had ignored the actions of the Sanctuary Movement. As the number of persons smuggled across the border by the underground railroad increased and as more church networks offered them sanctuary, news media coverage brought the issue to public attention and the INS began to arrest and prosecute those involved in the movement. In the first months of 1985, indictments and felony charges were filed against members of the Sanctuary Movement in different parts of the country because of the widespread support and publicity that the movement had received nationwide. That level of publicity forced the federal government to re-evaluate its refugee policy, and it began to take a closer look at the individual refugees' cases coming into the immigration court system.

In January 1985, a federal grand jury handed down a 71-count indictment against Corbett, Fife, and 14 other Sanctuary Movement leaders. The charges included conspiracy, smuggling, aiding, and harboring illegal aliens. After a six-month trial Jim Corbett was acquitted, but Rev. John Fife and six other sanctuary workers were sentenced to five years probation, and three others received three years in prison.

During this time many cities began to pass sanctuary laws as a way to help Central American refugees living in their communities. The sanctuary laws established new policies and practices that their local police departments had to follow when they arrested an undocumented immigrant. Historically, the local police departments cooperated very closely with INS officers, and after an undocumented immigrant was arrested, the individual would be turned over to immigration officials to be processed for deportation. The sanctuary laws no longer allowed the local police to work with INS officers during immigration raids and also prevented the police from turning over undocumented prisoners to INS officials for deportation. The sanctuary laws were designed to protect the safety of the undocumented immigrants and to develop better relations between police departments and the undocumented immigrant community. Many of the laws were drafted and passed after religious communities and Salvadoran and Latino community leaders organized lobbying efforts to have their municipal governments address the issues affecting Central American refugees. San Francisco, Berkeley, San Jose, San Diego, and Los Angeles in California were a few of the leading cities in helping pass the sanctuary legislation. New York City, Chicago, Houston, Portland, Miami, and Denver also passed similar legislation.

The Sanctuary Laws are presently under attack in response to the September 11, 2001, terrorist attacks in New York and Washington, D.C. In October 2002, U.S. Attorney General John Ashcroft, while addressing the International Association of Chiefs of Police convention in Billings, Montana, said the government will use all lawful means to prevent terrorism in this country. He assured the police chiefs that federal agents will investigate any cases brought to their attention by local law enforcement. Ashcroft expressed hope that an atmosphere of cooperation would help improve Homeland Security's efforts to protect the nation. Immigration advocates disagree with Ashcroft on what they perceive as an overzealous persecution of undocumented immigrants. Community leaders point out the recently leaked internal Justice Department report on the detention of illegal immigrants as a reason for not cooperating with immigration officials. They oppose the Justice Department's USA PATRIOT Act, which gives federal authorities broad sweeping powers to violate the Constitution in the pursuit of terrorists. They contend that the report revealed that most detainees had no known ties to terrorist groups, whatever their legal status.

The vague wording of the USA PATRIOT Act provides for multiple violations of the Constitution's Bill of Rights. For example, law enforcement agencies are now allowed to conduct "sneak and peek" searches of peoples' homes if they are suspected of terrorist activity. Police officers can break in, examine, remove, or alter items without informing the suspect. It also allows the Federal Bureau of Investigation (FBI) to obtain permission to look at parts of phone calls, emails, and internet communications by claiming that the information is "relevant to a criminal investigation." For immigrants, documented or undocumented, it allows for the indefinite detention of persons suspected of terrorist activity, with no requirement that the immigrants be given a trial or hearing in which the government would have to prove that they are actually terrorists.

THE IMPACT OF THE IMMIGRATION REFORM ACT OF 1986 ON SALVADORAN IMMIGRANTS

Beginning in May 1987, Congress legalized the amnesty provisions of the IRCA. This amnesty program granted legal status to undocumented persons who had entered and resided continuously in the United States territory prior to January 1, 1982. Originally, the INS estimated that more than 4 million eligible persons would apply for the program at the national level. At the end of the final application period, on May 5, 1988, a much smaller number of applicants had come forward to petition for legalization under the amnesty provisions. Only 1.4 million persons applied at the national level. The main factor for the low application numbers was a fear and distrust of the INS in the Latino communities throughout the country. Critics noted that the extensive paperwork to be filed, the lack of public education and outreach, and the restrictive regulations forced many persons not to apply for the program.

In the case of undocumented Salvadorans in the United States, it was clear that many people would not qualify for amnesty because of their arrival dates. One of the peaks of the migration waves of undocumented Salvadorans took place around 1982–83. These individuals did not qualify for the amnesty legalization provisions. It is estimated that most of the undocumented Salvadoran population arrived between 1982 and 1989, at the height of the civil war. Arriving in the country after the legalization deadlines, they could not obtain legal permanent residency and were not able to obtain work permits under the new immigration laws.

Table 2.2
Regular Provision Legalization Applicants from EL Salvador (I-6870) Immigration Reform and Control Act of 1986

Occupations	Total
All occupations	141,785
Professional specialty and technical	2.003
Architects	7
Engineers, surveyors, and mapping scientists	85
Math and computer scientists	3
Natural scientists	7
Health diagnosing professions	31
Doctors	10
Others	21
Health assessment and treatment occupations	681
Nurses	209
Others	472
Teachers, post-secondary	30
Teachers, except post-secondary	95
Counselors, educational/vocational	27
Librarians/archivists/curators	2
Social scientists/urban planners	2
Social/recreation/religious wo rkers	74
Lawyers	5
Writers/artists/entertainers/athletes	412
Health technologists/technicians	109
Technologists/technicians except health	433
Executive/administrative/managerial occupations	3,102
Sales occupations	3,826
Administrative support, including clerical	5,340
Precision production/craft/repair occupations	16,971

(*Continued*)

**Table 2.2
(continued)**

Occupations	Total
Operators/fabricators/laborers	32,559
Farming/forestry/fishing occupations	2,362
Service occupations	44,370
No occupation	21,850
Homemaker	3,005
Unemployed/retired	5,086
Students and/or children under 16	13,759
unknown or not reported	9,400

Source: Data compiled from the Statistical Handbook on U.S. Hispanics.

According to INS reports, by 1988 only 132,633 undocumented Salvadoran applicants for legalization had entered the country before the January 1, 1982, cutoff date. A total of 163,494 undocumented Salvadorans applied for the amnesty program and 21,709 undocumented Salvadorans applied for the Special Agricultural Worker Provisions (SAW). Most of the Salvadoran applicants were laborers in factories, service workers, students, or children younger than 16 years of age. Only a small percentage of all the Salvadoran applicants had professional status or a technical occupation (Table 2.2).

TEMPORARY PROTECTED STATUS FOR SALVADORANS

Temporary Protected Status (TPS) was originally presented to the U.S. Congress as a proposal in 1983 and was denied at the time. The proposal was presented for a second time in 1986 and was again denied. Then in November 1990, after four years of lobbying Congress, the law was passed and signed as part of the Immigration Act of 1990. The Attorney General may designate a country for TPS classification as a provisional immigration status if (1) there is an ongoing armed conflict within the country that poses a serious threat to the personal safety of its citizens if they were required to return; (2) there has been a natural disaster such as an earthquake, flood, or drought, or environmental disaster resulting in the disruption of the living conditions; (3) the country is unable to handle the return of its citizens and has officially requested TPS designation; and (4) other exceptional circumstances make return to the country unsafe, and temporary asylum in the United States is not against the national interest of the United States.

El Salvador was one of the few countries that was certified for consideration for TPS and designated Salvadoran nationals residing in the United States since September 19, 1990, as eligible for TPS. Temporary Protected Status was granted for only an 18-month period that began January 1, 1991. Deportation proceedings were suspended while the individuals were under the TPS program. At that time, the INS estimated that between 120,000 and 150,000 Salvadorans would apply for TPS by the registration deadline of October 31, 1991. Individuals qualified for TPS if they had been living continuously in the United States since the effective date of designation; had been continuously living in the United States since a date set by the Attorney General; were admissible as an immigrant; and had not been convicted of a felony or two or more misdemeanors in the United States. The Attorney General has to determine that the described person has not persecuted others, committed particular serious crimes or other nonpolitical crimes, and does not pose a danger to the national security.

DEFERRED ENFORCED DEPARTURE

After the 18 months expired for the original TPS category in October 1991, an extension was requested from Congress. The Department of Justice granted the extension for an additional 12 months, but only to Salvadorans already living in the United States. This new category of TPS for Salvadorans became known as Temporary Protected Status/Deferred Enforced Departure (TPS/DED). An additional extension was requested and was in effect until December 1994. Those individuals residing in the United States under the TPS/DED category were denied any additional extensions, but their work permits remained valid until September 30, 1995. After that date, they were expected to voluntarily leave U.S. territory and return to El Salvador.

The attorney general once again designated El Salvador as a country qualifying for TPS in March 2001, after a series of severe earthquakes left more than one-fourth of the country's population without adequate housing, and the designation was subsequently extended. Only one third of 170,000 homes that were destroyed by the earthquakes have been rebuilt. More than three quarters of the damaged roads have not been repaired or replaced. Salvadorans once again have received this provisional immigration status, are not required to leave the United States, and may obtain employment authorization during the designated period of the TPS. The authority to make TPS designations has now been transferred from the attorney general to the Secretary of Homeland Security as part of the recent legislation that created that department, and the secretary decided to extend the designation for El Salvador until 2006. The official notice explains that the economy of El Salvador is not yet stable enough to absorb returnees from the United States should TPS not be extended. In addition, a large number of Salvadoran returnees from the United States would not be able to find appropriate housing or employment opportunities, and that may add to the social unrest, the critical crime situation, and the dismal living conditions present in El Salvador.

To register for the extension, Salvadoran nationals previously granted TPS must have been continuously physically present in the United States since March 9, 2001; or they must have resided in the United States on or before February 13, 2001, and have continuously resided in the United States until the present; the individual must also be admissible as an immigrant and have no criminal or security-related record barring him or her from living in this country. Individuals must have reapplied for the new TPS designation during the registration period that began on July 16, 2003, and ended on September 15, 2003, in order to qualify for it. The Department of Homeland Security estimates that 290,000 Salvadorans will continue to benefit from living and working in the United States.

AMERICAN BAPTIST CHURCH—POLITICAL ASYLUM

The legal case known as *American Baptist Churches v. Thornburg,* 760 F. Supp 796 (N.D. Cal. 1991) has played an important role in the lives of many Central American refugees in the United States. This case (ABC) was filed in May 1985 on behalf of more than 80 religious and refugee assistance organizations that claimed that the INS and the State Department had a history of discriminatory practices against Salvadorans and Guatemalans applying for political asylum. The case was settled on January 31, 1991, and it was applied to Salvadorans who were residing in the United States as of September 19, 1990. As a result of this decision, individuals who had been denied political asylum by a district director, an immigration judge, or the Board of Immigration Appeals could get another opportunity to have their cases reviewed by a new trained corps of asylum officers hired under the regulations in effect in October 1990. Moreover, the INS could only detain class members eligible for relief who were subject to arrest by applicable laws and who had been convicted of a crime involving moral turpitude with a sentence exceeding six months; or that they posed a threat to the national security or public safety. The INS was given the authority to detain individuals who were likely to hide after their cases were denied.

Many Salvadorans who feared that TPS or TPS/DED was a short-term remedy for their immigration status actually became interested and applied for the ABC political asylum process. These individuals were interested in a more permanent solution than TPS/DED because they feared for their personal safety upon their return to El Salvador. These individuals needed to meet the criteria to qualify for political asylum. Approximately 50,000 Guatemalans and Salvadorans registered in 1991.

For more than 10 years, political asylum applications in the United States came mostly from Central American nationals. Central Americans filed approximately half of the political asylum applications submitted between 1986 and 1992. The numbers declined to about 40 percent by 1994, and then went up substantially until 1996. By early 1997, the numbers demonstrated a sharp decline, owing to the ending of the filing dates of the ABC settlement. During the 1990s, most of the asylum claims by Salvadorans and other Central Americans were influenced by the ABC cases. Under this 1991 class action suit, Salvadorans and Guatemalans were able to file or renew their cases for asylum. The 187,000 Salvadorans who had registered for TPS became eligible to file for political asylum after their TPS expired in 1992. An extension was granted to Salvadorans until January 31, 1996, to apply for asylum under the ABC agreement.

At the end of the ABC application period, the numbers sharply declined and by 2002 only about 2 percent of all political asylum claims were filed by Central Americans. Also, the civil war ended in El Salvador in 1992 and Salvadorans found it difficult to meet the requirements of political asylum as the country was expected to be in a state of peace.

On November 19, 1997, the NACARA permitted Salvadorans, Guatemalans, and Nicaraguans to apply for the suspension of deportation or special rule cancellation of removal under the more generous standards in effect before the 1996 Immigration Law. Those individuals that qualified for relief under NACARA were allowed to remain in the United States as lawful permanent residents. Cases filed by nationals of El Salvador (49 percent of total pending) and Guatemala accounted for about 79 percent of the pending cases at the end of September 2002. The ABC cases, which can be handled under the NACARA provisions, made up 98 percent of the Salvadoran and 95 percent of Guatemalan cases filed, and 76 percent of all pending cases as of the end of September 2002.

CITIZENSHIP EFFORTS

One of the important areas of immediate concern and action is citizenship drives. It is imperative for Salvadoran immigrants who plan to live in the United States to become U.S. naturalized citizens as the means of empowering the Salvadoran immigrant communities. In the past many immigrants have not wanted to become naturalized U.S. citizens because of their ethnic loyalties. They did not want to "betray" their national origin and citizenship by giving up their identity and nationality as Salvadorans. In recent years, the Salvadoran government has passed legislation that permits its citizens to hold a dual citizenship. Table 2.3 shows the numbers of Salvadorans who became naturalized U.S. citizens from 1979–2002.

In recent years, as a result of the anti-immigrant hysteria affecting the United States, Proposition 187, and HR Bill 999, many social services and programs traditionally available to immigrants became more restricted and are only available to U.S. citizens. When proposition 187 in California was enacted by the voters and affirmed by the courts in 1994, it restricted essential social and medical services to U.S. citizens only. Proposition 187 prohibited public social services for non-U.S. citizens, lawful permanent residents, or aliens who have been lawfully admitted temporarily. Only persons who meet the previous criteria may receive health care services from a publicly funded health care facility, other than emergency medical care as required by federal law. Anyone else must be denied the requested services or other benefits, directed in writing to either obtain legal status or leave the United States and be reported to the authorities, including the INS.

Proposition 187 also limited enrollment in public schools to U.S. citizens and to aliens lawfully admitted to the United States for permanent residence or otherwise authorized to be here. The law gave school districts until January 1, 1995 to verify the status of pupils and their parents; but whenever they reasonably suspect a violation they have only 45 days to notify INS and other authorities and to advise parents that schooling will be cut off in 90 days. The impact of Proposition 187 was felt almost immediately in the Latino communities of California, and it created a strong political movement among Latinos who organized a series of extremely effective citizenship drives as the means of empowering Latinos and forcing legislators to represent the interests of Latinos in California and the rest of the nation. This situation is quite evident in the Salvadoran communities across the country, as Salvadorans took action and began to process their citizenship papers after the passage of proposition 187. Large numbers of Salvadorans have become citizens since then. According to INS data, 29,327 Salvadoran immigrants became

Table 2.3
Salvadorans Naturalized as Citizens in the
United States by Year, 1979–2002

Year	Numbers	Year	Numbers
1979	770	1991	3,653
1980	988	1992	2,056
1981	1,252	1993	3,038
1982	1,187	1994	5,643
1983	1,126	1995	13,702
1984	1,380	1996	35,478
1985	2,119	1997	18,273
1986	2,628	1998	12,267
1987	2,428	1999	22,991
1988	2,291	2000	24,073
1989	2,001	2001	13,663
1990	2,410	2002	10,716

Source: Statistical Yearbooks of the INS 1993–2002.

naturalized U.S. citizens between 1979 and 1994. Between 1994 and 2002, 156,806 Salvadorans became citizens. In the two-year period after the passage of Proposition 187 almost 50,000 Salvadorans became citizens. Other anti-immigrant legislation that impacted Salvadorans was HR Bill 999. This bill cut welfare to immigrant mothers and does not allow educational financial aid to be awarded to noncitizen students. It also restricts other youth programs in inner-city working-class communities. This anti-immigrant climate has had an impact on the Latino and specifically in the Salvadoran communities. Many community organizations have successfully organized citizenship drives and voter registration drives to counterattack this type of legislation. In California, the Central American Resource Centers (CARECEN) launched extremely successful citizenship drives that resulted in large numbers of Salvadorans becoming naturalized citizens. Thousands of people showed up for informational workshops to help them with the process and paperwork necessary to becoming a U.S. citizen.

But the programs did not end only in citizenship drives, as Salvadoran communities became empowered by helping the new citizens to register to vote and to teach them to participate in the electoral campaigns at the local, state, and national levels. This has been an opportunity that Salvadoran immigrants, now citizens, have used to advocate for Salvadoran and Latino issues, and they now have a right and the means to determine the future of Salvadorans in the United States.

NOTES

1. American Civil Liberties Union. *Salvadorans in the United States: The Case for Extended Voluntary Departure.* (Washington, D.C.: National Immigration and Alien Rights Project, Report No. 1, April 1984).

2. National Lawyers Guild. *Immigration Law and Defense.* (New York: Clark Boardman Company and ACLU, 1984)s.

3. American Civil Liberties Union, *Salvadorans in the United States,* 1984.

4. Boyd Caroli, "Recent Immigration to the United States," in *Ethnic and Immigration Groups: The United States, Canada and England,* ed. P.J.F. Rosof, W. Zeizel, J. B. Quandt, and M. Maayan (New York: Haworth Press, 1983), 49–69.

5. M. E. Gettleman, P. Lacefield, L. Menashe, D. Mermelstein, and R. Radosh (eds.), *El Salvador: Central America in the New Cold War* (New York: Grove Press, 1981).

3

Causes of Salvadoran and Central American Emigration and Waves of Migration

MIGRATION DETERMINANTS

Various social, economic, political, and cultural factors influence individuals' decisions to migrate and relocate to a new area of residence. Migration movements from El Salvador to the United States have taken place at various times since the early years of the twentieth century, and each migration movement has its own characteristics based on the economic, social, and political conditions present in El Salvador and the United States at that moment in history. The Salvadoran emigration processes during the 1980s were caused by the political climate of El Salvador, or "la situación," as Salvadorans called it. This is an ambiguous term frequently used by Salvadorans to describe the sociopolitical reality of El Salvador, without expressing clear and concrete accounts of the extent of their personal involvement in the political crisis. After further questioning and establishing a feeling of confidence and trust, the Salvadorans may elaborate specific details of the events that forced them to leave their country. Most Salvadorans who came to the United States during this time have expressed that they would not have left El Salvador if the sociopolitical conflict did not exist and that when the political conditions were to become favorable they would be willing to return to live or to visit the country.

War and Revolution

The migration of Salvadorans to the United States between 1979 and the late 1990s has been motivated mostly by political and economic factors influenced by the civil war that ravaged that Central American nation between 1979 and 1992. One of the main characteristics of this migration wave was the involuntary or forced character of the population movements out of El Salvador during this period of time. This migration wave also had both direct and indirect political determinants.

Most Salvadorans who left their country during the 1980s fall into the following classifications of reasons for leaving Central America:

1. Some individuals left El Salvador as a consequence of being involved in political activities. They had an active membership in political parties or organizations; some were members of the military or revolutionary organizations or members of labor unions. Many of them were arrested, abducted, and/or tortured, or attempts against their lives were made by Salvadoran security forces or paramilitary death squads. These are individuals who actively participated in political parties and labor, agricultural, and teacher unions such as the Christian Democrat Party, Farm Worker Unions, and the National Association of Salvadoran Educators (ANDES). Other individuals who were forced to leave were Catholic or Protestant catechizers. They were common targets of paramilitary groups, because they were labeled as subversives or communists due to their practice of Liberation Theology. Employment in specific fields or residence in specific geographic or socioeconomic communities in El Salvador was considered subversive and individuals became direct targets for political violence.

2. Other Salvadorans had indirect political reasons for leaving their country. There was a great deal of uncontrolled or selective political violence against specific groups. During this period there was a great deal of institutionalized violence and violations of human rights in the civilian population. Some people received death threats against themselves or their families from paramilitary killing squads, because of involvement, activism, or membership in labor unions, academic circles, or religious associations.

3. Some were forced to emigrate after receiving death threats from Leftist guerrillas due to their personal or family involvement in right-wing political parties, government agencies, military service, or paramilitary organizations.

4. Some were forced to emigrate because they had relatives who had been assassinated by the Right or the Left. It is often assumed that the families of political activists are targets of political violence.

5. Administrators, faculty, staff, and students of the National University were often considered targets for political persecution by the security forces and paramilitary organizations. During the early 1980s, many students migrated to the United States and abroad after the university was militarized and closed for more than four years. The government has considered the university the breeding grounds for political activism; it has historically been a target of government repression.

6. A large percentage of the population was displaced because of the military activity in rural El Salvador. Many towns were under government military control and the population was forcibly relocated to refugee camps. Many of these individuals were unable to find jobs and feared for their personal safety. Many were farm laborers with little education who relocated in the agricultural regions of the southwestern United States rather than in the metropolitan centers.

7. Finally, some individuals left El Salvador because they considered it dangerous to remain in the country. They were afraid of getting caught in the crossfire of the political violence because of the nature of their employment, area of residence, and/or age.

Some individuals may have been motivated to emigrate from El Salvador to the United States for more than one reason. It is obvious that whatever influenced their migration, Salvadorans were affected either directly or indirectly by the sociopolitical and military conflict. The civil war affected everyone living in El Salvador, and even those who were not politically involved suffered the consequences. There are very narrow political definitions used in the country. One is either on one side or the other. There is no middle ground.

Economic Migrations

The migration of Salvadorans to the United States before 1979 and after the late 1990s has been motivated mostly by economic factors. These economic migrations may be both voluntary as well as involuntary based on a variety of factors.

Immigrants who make a conscious decision to migrate because of economic reasons experience the same type of migration stresses manifested in recently arrived immigrants who were forced to leave. They suffer from culture shock, but their cultural adaptation and socialization experiences tend to be less stressful than those who are forced to migrate. This type of voluntary migration may involve family reunification, which is a happy event. The decision to migrate is always made by the heads of the family, and children do not always participate in the decision-making process. Children often do not feel that their migration is of a voluntary nature since the elders in the family made the decisions.

Those who are part of the "brain drain phenomenon"—the highly skilled workers and professionals— may have left El Salvador voluntarily. Significant numbers of Salvadoran professionals migrated to the United States before 1979 and established themselves in Latino communities in Los Angeles, San Francisco, Houston, New York, and Washington, D.C. They paved the way for others that would follow during the Civil War and thereafter.

Economic migrations are highly influenced by push/pull factors as they create circular migration circuits. The push factors are created by societies with a weak economic system that is dominated by the international world market demands. Such is the case in El Salvador, where the economy is completely dependent on the U.S. economy and has high unemployment rates with very limited employment opportunities for its citizens. The pull factors, on the other hand, are highly influenced by the stable economic systems and low unemployment rates of the industrialized nations. Salvadoran immigrants are motivated to pursue the opportunities available in the United States where there is an ample supply of low-paying jobs available for unskilled workers. These low wages are relative compared with the wages and employment opportunities available in El Salvador for many workers, and the benefits are much greater in the United States than those at home.

But not all economic migrations are of a voluntary nature. An economic migration may also be involuntary. For example, after the closing down of a factory or the like, and at times when the local economy may be weak, Salvadoran workers might not have any real employment possibilities. Therefore, the only option available to them may be to migrate to the United States and join family members or friends in search of better employment opportunities. In addition, natural catastrophes such as earthquakes, hurricanes, drought, or floods may destroy parts of the economic infrastructure and force people to leave their country in search of better economic opportunities abroad.

Today, the Salvadoran economy is undergoing difficult times. After the terrorist attacks in the United States on September 11, 2001, the world economic system suffered a severe blow, investments went down, tourism to many parts of the world was almost paralyzed, and oil prices began to rapidly increase. The Salvadoran economy, which is highly dependent on the U.S. investments, was critically affected by the economic impact of the terrorist attacks. As a result, many businesses had to fold, their workers, in turn, were not able to find jobs and were forced to seek better opportunities outside the country. Most of the displaced workers have migrated to Salvadoran communities in the United States with the hope of finding employment and helping their families back in Central America.

ARRIVING IN THE UNITED STATES

To fully analyze the social, cultural, and political experiences of Salvadoran populations in the United States, it is important to get a clear understanding of the various definitions of Central America. The most accepted definition of the region includes Guatemala, El Salvador, Honduras, Nicaragua, and Costa Rica. These countries share a common pre-Hispanic, Spanish colonial, and post-colonial history, which includes economic, political, social, and cultural traditions. These countries were part of the Central American United Provinces created at the time of the Spanish independence period and have had held a close common cultural history since pre-Hispanic times.

Other more recent perspectives of the definition of the region are founded on geographic, commercial, and economic factors, and these definitions also include the countries of Belize and Panama. For the purposes here, the more traditional definition will be used. Central Americans are proud of their national origins and strongly believe in and practice the philosophy of Pan Americanism. In Latin America the definition of "America" refers not only to the United States but is also inclusive of all the countries in the continent from North to South, plus the Caribbean region.

For more than a century, Central Americans have continuously immigrated into the United States as a result of a number of social, political, and economic factors and numerous natural disasters that have plagued the region. The Central American countries vary greatly in size, geography, history, political systems, ethnic make-up, linguistic traditions, levels of urbanization and industrialization, as well as the numbers of their immigrant populations who have resettled in the United States. Immigrants from these countries have been incorporated into the social fabric of the United States in different ways. In many instances, the U.S. government has welcomed some groups more than others. Although most Central Americans are Spanish speakers, the population also includes different indigenous populations who speak their own native languages and are culturally different from the mainstream populations in their countries. Guatemala and Honduras have a large population of Mayan peoples who speak Quiché, Mam, Kechki, Kanjobal, or any of the other Mayan languages. In Honduras and Nicaragua there are indigenous peoples who speak Miskitu, Sumo, or Rama languages, and there are other Central Americans from the Atlantic Coast who speak English. Racially and ethnically, Central Americans are the descendants of indigenous Indian, African, and European people; the population also includes people of Asian, Jewish, Arab, and other European origins. Although most Central Americans are Roman Catholic, there are also many Protestants and a smaller number of Jews and people of other faiths. Indigenous peoples have continued to practice their ancient native religions that have been blended with European Roman Catholicism.

Central American Immigration Patterns to the United States

Migration waves have been defined as the rises, peaks, and declines in population movements, as they reflect the economic, social, and political conditions of both the United States and national origin of the immigrant population.[1] This definition is practical in the analysis of the history of Central American migrations to the United States. Central Americans have settled in the United States since the late 1800s. Since the early twentieth century, various small migration waves of Salvadorans have arrived.

Those migration waves were not significantly large until recently. The INS only began to keep detailed records of Central American migrations after 1932. Between 1820 and 2003, the INS reported that more than one million immigrants from Central America had legally resettled in the United States. More than half of the Central American immigrant population settled in the United States after 1980. The post-1980s Central American migration waves have also included a very large number of undocumented persons. As a result of the unclear immigration policies and practices regarding Central Americans in effect before 1965, the numbers on record appear to be extremely low. For example, Salvadoran consular records estimated that by the early 1970s there was already a population of about 40,000 living in the San Francisco Bay Area, but INS records indicate a much lower figure at the national level.

The First Central American Migration Wave (1870–1930)

The first wave of Central American immigration to the United States can be traced to the late 1800s when coffee was introduced as a cash crop in Central America and a thriving export trade developed in the West Coast with San Francisco as the chief processing center. Central Americans began to arrive in the San Francisco Bay Area as part of labor contracts and business contracts with many of the local coffee or banana companies that conducted business and owned property in El Salvador and the rest of Central America. These coffee companies included MJB, Hills Brothers, and Folgers. Once these links were established, the foundations of various social migration networks were created and led to migratory movements back and forth between the United States and Central America, at first limited to the Central American elite. But gradually, many Central Americans, both male and female, were recruited to work in coffee factories and other industries in California. Central Americans who worked for the banana companies often relocated in New York or New Orleans.

The Second Central American Migration Wave (1930–1941)

The second wave of Central American immigration to the United States occurred during the 1930s. The economic crisis and political instability that affected Latin America in the 1930s created the right conditions for the first significantly large Central American migrations to the United States. During the 1930s the Central American military attained high levels of control in the government and began to share political and economic power with the oligarchic families that had ruled most Central American countries since the 1860s. In Nicaragua, for example, the military under the leadership of General Anastasio Somoza García created one of the most repressive dictatorships in Central America and forced large numbers of Nicaraguans to leave the country. Somoza García in Nicaragua and Maximiliano Hernández Martínez in El Salvador ruled their countries with an iron hand and did not allow for dissidents to express themselves. It was common for the military to issue an ultimatum to a dissident, place the person and the family under house arrest, and soon after force the family into exile. They were allowed to take with them only the things that they could carry in their hands, and quite often high-ranking officers in the military kept the assets and belongings for their own personal use. This cohort of Central American immigrants comprised men and women from the urban middle and upper classes who had relatively high levels of education—intellectuals, teachers, labor organizers, political dissidents, and exiled military officers who were not in agreement with their national governments. There were also individuals who had direct ties to their governments and/or who were members of the dominant social class in their country. Their migration was motivated by their desire to escape failing economies, political persecution, and lack of personal freedoms.

For the first time, a significant population of Central Americans began to resettle in the San Francisco Bay Area, New York, and Los Angeles. Nicaraguans became the largest Central American immigrant group and started to develop the social and economic foundations for the Nicaraguan and Salvadoran ethnic communities in the United States. Many of these new immigrants found employment in the U.S. industrial sectors. Men often worked as longshoremen or in construction while women found work in the textile and shipping industries.

The Third Central American Migration Wave (1941–1950)

With the significant demand for labor during World War II, many Central Americans went to work in Panama, where there was an economic boom because of the high traffic of ships and commerce in the Panama Canal Zone. Large numbers of Salvadorans went to Panama to seek their fortune and with the hope of getting a labor contract in the United States, and many distinguished themselves as good workers and eventually received labor contracts in the United States. They would make the journey on a California-bound ship and relocate in Los Angeles or San Francisco. With the high labor demands of the industrial military economy during World War II, many Central Americans found jobs in the United States. Both men and women were able to easily find work in various industries, especially in the shipping and naval yards, as well as in the textile industry.[2]

Central American immigrants during this time resettled in established Latin American communities in New York, San Francisco, Los Angeles, Houston, and New Orleans. They revitalized the cultural, social, and economic life in the small Central American ethnic communities and neighborhoods that had already been established during the past two decades.

Unlike subsequent waves of Central American immigrants, this third wave of Central American immigrants relied not only on the labor contracts but also on extended family networks established by the first waves of immigrants. Future migration waves would also rely on ethnic, neighborhood, village, or national migration networks. It was this cohort of Central American immigrants who became active members of social migration networks and helped to establish the social and religious communities and economic foundations of U.S.-based Latin American immigrant communities that would benefit future generations of Central Americans and other Latin Americans who arrived later.

This migration wave had an interesting characteristic in that a significant number of Salvadorans and Nicaraguans returned to live permanently in Central America. Many Central American immigrant workers found themselves competing for job opportunities with the returning service men who had fought overseas. As the service men returned, the job market became more difficult for immigrants and many Central Americans decided to permanently return to their native countries.

During the 1950s, the returning migrants became part of a new aspiring industrial and commercial economic force in El Salvador and the rest of Central America. They managed to save their earnings while working in the United States and then invested in innovative economic enterprises that rapidly introduced the local societies to U.S. technology and material culture.

Such was the case of the Eva family who had arrived in San Francisco from Rivass, Nicaragua during the late 1930s. Two Eva brothers, José and Vicente, who were expert craftsmen who made fine furniture and cabinets, came first. On their arrival in San Francisco, they began to work in a funeral home making caskets. They distinguished themselves on the job and were able to adjust quite well to life in the city. The two brothers began to bring other family members to join them and to work with them. After World War II, the funeral business experienced a decline, so the Eva brothers decided to return to Nicaragua. There they applied all of the new things that they had learned from the funeral business to their new project. They introduced to the Nicaraguan population a new type of funeral insurance and funeral services based on the U.S. model, and their business became one of the most successful enterprises in the region for the next 40 years. It was so successful that they expanded to El Salvador, Honduras, Costa Rica, and Panama. They were able to use their carpentry skills and innovations learned in San Francisco for a new approach to business that had never been seen in Central America until then.

The immigrants who remained in the United States after World War II continued to develop the economic and social foundations of the Latino ethnic enclaves and ethnic communities. They worked together with other Latino groups such as Puerto Ricans and Mexicans and created many ethnic coalitions to achieve these goals.

The Fourth Central American Migration Wave (1960–1970)

The fourth wave of Central American immigration to the United States took place in the 1960s when more than 100,000 Central Americans legally became permanent resident aliens. Before 1965, according to the U.S. Census, approximately 57,737 Central Americans resided in the United States. In the mid-1960s, Central American immigration to the United States began to increase dramatically. The increase was influenced by the Immigration Act of 1965, passed during the Johnson administration, which allowed numerous young working-class and middle-class Central American families to resettle in the United States. These new immigration policies allowed for the granting of immigrant quotas to countries that historically had not been included. Newcomers resettled in established Latin American neighborhoods in U.S. cities with their social networks, familiar cultural traditions, and support systems that had been developed and maintained by the Latin American immigrants since the 1930s. The new Central American arrivals further developed the economic, social, and cultural structures of the Latin American communities in San Francisco, Los Angeles, Houston, New York, New Jersey, New Orleans, and Washington, D.C.

The Fifth Central American Migration Wave (1975–1990)

The influx of Central American immigrants to the United States demonstrated a sharp increase since the 1970s. In the late 1970s and early 1980s, migration patterns from Central America changed as a direct result of sociopolitical and socioeconomic conditions in the region. Political turmoil and revolutionary movements in Central America forced large numbers of Salvadorans, Guatemalans, Nicaraguans, and Hondurans to enter the United States as political asylum applicants or without legal immigration documentation. While the pre-1979 migrations were mostly economic in nature, the post-1979 migrations were generated by the political stresses and the severe economic conditions faced by most of Central America.

The Central American political climate began to heat up in the mid-1970s as a number of insurgent movements started to challenge the established governments in the political and military arenas. The Frente Sandinista de Liberación Nacional (FSLN) in Nicaragua, various guerrilla organizations in Guatemala, and electoral fraud in El Salvador became significant factors and determinant forces that shaped up the migration dynamics of the Central American population. Undocumented migration patterns to the United States become more evident as political and economic instability escalated throughout the region.

In Nicaragua, the Sandinista revolution was in full combat against the government led by General Anastasio Somoza Debayle by mid-1977. Young men and women who fought to end the 45-year rule by the Somoza family composed the rank and file of the FSLN guerrilla organization. As a result, young people became a direct target of repression and persecution by the government's National Guard. The National Guard tent forced a military conscription of young civilians who were considered to be subversive elements in society. Large numbers of young people arrived in the United States after the Somoza government began a massive attack that involved the indiscriminate bombings of civilian populations by the Air Force and National Guard in the largest Nicaraguan cities. Numerous families and unaccompanied young men and women sought refuge in California, Florida, and New York to escape the political violence.

After the success of the Sandinista Revolution in Nicaragua, an interesting new migration dynamic began to appear in the region. Many families that had lived for decades in the United States and sympathized with the Sandinistas returned at this time to live in Nicaragua and to participate in the new social experiment being carried out by the Sandinistas. However, many families living in Nicaragua that disagreed with the Sandinista ideology and government platform decided to leave Nicaragua and started to relocate in the United States. They arrived in Miami, New York, Los Angeles, and the San Francisco Bay Area in the early 1980s. As in most cases when immigrants are forced out of their homeland by leftist revolutionary movements, the new arrivals in the United States tended to be more conservative than their predecessors and brought with them substantial sums of money that they invested in business and real estate enterprises in the Central American enclaves in the United States. Many of the new arrivals were wealthier and better educated. A large number of them had actually been educated in the United States and were fluent in English and highly familiar with U.S. culture. These new immigrants changed the ideological foundations of Central American communities in the United States.

In the late 1980s in El Salvador, the Frente Farabundo Martí para la Liberación Nacional (FMLN) escalated its armed insurgency campaign against the conservative oligarchy and the military and civilian governments. Amnesty International and other human rights organizations reported that between 1980 and 1983, right-wing paramilitary death squads assassinated more than 55,000 people in El Salvador. The people targeted for assassination were labor leaders, intellectuals, professionals, organizers, Catholic priests, lay workers, and anyone who attempted to change the social system. Salvadoran society had been seriously impacted by a long history of political corruption, and the civil war affected the social realities of the country. The judicial system was not able to offer protection to civilians. Threats and intimidation prevented justice and personal freedoms to exist. Furthermore, the violence in Salvadoran society reflected war, political violence and repression, as well as the breakdown of law and order. Civilians were in serious danger during both the counter-insurgency operations of the government and the guerrilla campaigns.

In areas of conflict, the civilian population was forcedly removed and relocated in refugee camps throughout El Salvador and in other Central American countries. The refugees were often subjected to the government's anti-insurgency campaigns that resulted in the massacres of elderly, women, and children, who made up the vast majority of the refugee population. Civilians were often caught in the crossfire of the civil war. A narrow definition of political activities existed in El Salvador during that period; an individual was either a subversive or a government sympathizer. As a result, many civilians were abducted, tortured, or killed by paramilitary death squads based on their political, social, or religious associations. The unsafe political climate displaced large numbers of people and influenced the migration from El Salvador to other Central American countries, South America, the United States, Canada, Europe, and Australia. The prestigious Colegio de Mexico conducted a study for the United Nations and the Mexican government; they found that the Salvadoran migration to Mexico was motivated by fear of political repression. The study concluded that it was impossible to determine whether the Salvadorans who continued their journey to the United States were mainly interested in political and social freedoms or simply wanted to enjoy better job opportunities.[3]

Political instability, war, revolution, and their impact on the local economy were the main causes for Salvadorans to leave the Central American region. The Salvadoran Diasporas became active as new immigrants arrived on a daily basis to their new social environments. Salvadorans relocated in other Central American countries, either on their own or in refugee camps found in Honduras, Nicaragua, and Costa Rica. Others relocated in Venezuela, Mexico, Canada, the United States, France, Sweden, Spain, or Australia. The Salvadorans who came to the United States continued to relocate in communities that had a significant Latin American population so as to better adjust to their new cultural environment. Salvadorans followed different types of social migration networks; some followed a family, hometown, or an ethnic network where they found the necessary support systems for survival in the United States. In addition, most of these new immigrants arrived without the proper immigration status and documentation. During the early 1980s, Salvadorans established their new residence in Los Angeles, Washington D.C., New York, New Jersey, San Francisco, Houston, Boston, and Miami.

The Sixth Central American Migration Wave (1991–2004)

When Hurricane Mitch hit Central America at the end of October 1998, it left thousands dead and millions of people homeless. The governments of Guatemala, El Salvador, and Honduras were forced to face one of the most serious economic crises in recent years as the infrastructure was severely affected. For the affected poor, and specially the young, the only available option for survival was to migrate to the United States. The impact of the migration of these displaced persons has added more fuel to the ongoing immigration debate in the United States as more Central American immigrants continue to arrive.

Almost three years later, El Salvador was again hit by more natural disasters: two major earthquakes struck during January and February 2001. On January 13, 2001 an earthquake measuring 7.7 on the Richter scale killed at least 844 people, injured 4,723 people, destroyed 108,226 houses, and seriously damaged more than 150,000 buildings in El Salvador. Utilities and roads were damaged by more than 16,000 landslides. A month later, on February 13, 2001, another earthquake, measuring 6.6 on the Richter scale, hit El Salvador and caused a large number of landslides, destroying and damaging homes and severely damaging the rural water systems throughout the country. The earthquakes destroyed large sections of the capitol and its surrounding communities, and approximately 1.5 million Salvadorans were left without shelter. The earthquake further aggravated the Salvadoran economy and many more Salvadorans embarked on the journey north following the well-established social migration networks in Salvadoran and Central American communities and enclaves in the United States. The transnational impact of migration is so evident in the Central American countries that many villages in the Central American rural areas today know exactly when the apples are being picked in the valleys of Washington state or when hotels are hiring in Atlanta.[4]

In the past few years, Salvadorans and other Central Americans have continued migrating within the United States and are moving to areas that traditionally have been outside their target for settlement. Many are moving to the South, to places such as central Florida and Atlanta to pursue jobs in factories that are relocating in those regions; others are moving to Oklahoma to work in construction or agriculture. Some of the reasons stated by these immigrants for moving from Los Angeles, San Francisco, or any other large metropolitan areas are related to issues such as lack of employment opportunities, high cost of living, decaying school systems, youth gangs, and crime in the cities.

NOTES

1. Thomas Muller and Thomas Espenshade, *The Fourth Wave: California's Newest Immigrants* (Washington, D.C.: The Urban Institute Press, 1986).

2. The author conducted numerous ethnographic interviews with Central American immigrants in San Francisco and Los Angeles between 1980–2003 and addressed many of the issues related to their migration experiences. Different generations of immigrants were interviewed, and then provided a wealth of information related to their time of arrival as well as their experiences in the United States.

3. M. Fazlollah, "Fleeing Salvadorans: The Painful Journey North," *Migration Today*, XII, no. 2 (Summer 1984): 22–27.

4. Richard Rodriguez, "For the Poor, Movement is the Only Answer to Natural Disasters," *JINN Magazine* 4, no. 23 (November 9–22, 1998).

4

Demographics of Salvadorans and Other Central Americans in the United States

SALVADORAN POPULATIONS IN THE UNITED STATES SINCE 1979

Since 1979, the influx of Salvadoran immigrants to the United States has risen at a high rate. According to recent studies, most Salvadoran immigrants that arrived in the United States before 1979 came as legal permanent residents. Since 1979, the trend has changed significantly as large numbers of Salvadorans have entered the United States as undocumented immigrants and asylum seekers.

Furthermore, the pre-1979 migrations were mostly economic in nature, while the post-1979 migrations have been motivated largely by political and economic determinants as well as by natural disasters. Undocumented Salvadorans had been arriving in the United States since the early 1970s, but the numbers were not significant before then. As the economic, social, and political realities in El Salvador were impacted by political violence and civil war in the 1980s, more Salvadorans left their country and relocated throughout the newly created Salvadoran diasporas in neighboring Central American and Latin American countries, Mexico, the United States, and Canada. Others migrated to various countries in Europe, such as Spain, Sweden, France, and Italy. Others went as far as Australia, where there are important Salvadoran immigrant communities at this time.[1]

Central Americans arrived in large numbers in the United States during the 1980s seeking refuge from the civil wars, political persecution, and economic conditions that had been negatively impacted by the civil wars and political unrest. During the 1990s, the civil wars in Central America came to an end after the local governments and the leftist insurgents agreed upon Peace Accords. Even though the overt political violence had winded down by the mid-1990s, few Central American immigrants were making plans to permanently return to their countries. Many Salvadorans that came to the United States during the period of war continued to fear for their personal safety and that of their families if they returned to live in El Salvador. In addition, many Salvadorans either brought their children with them or have U.S.-born children now, and it would be extremely difficult for their children to adjust to a new lifestyle in El Salvador. After living in the United States for more than a decade, individuals have already well-established roots in the U.S. communities and no longer feel that they could adjust to life in El Salvador.

In many instances the parents are willing to return and live in El Salvador but their children are the ones that want to remain in the United States, as many of them have never been to their parent's native country. Salvadorans are very family oriented and in most cases, the elders in the family make the decision to remain in this country in order to maintain the integrity of the extended family unit. Another factor may be that their grown children have married outside the Salvadoran group and their spouses may not be so willing to experiment living in a place that they are not familiar with. It is very

Salvadoran family gathering. Photo by Carlos Texca.

difficult to adjust to life in El Salvador after having lived in the United States for a prolonged period of time; people get used to the cultural patterns and employment opportunities available to them in the United States. For individuals that were victims of the political persecution, repression, abductions, and torture, or had a close family member who was a victim of the horrors of the war, it is a very traumatic experience to try to return to a country that they no longer see as part of their present life but as a place of a nightmare that they want to erase from their memories.

During recent years Salvadorans, Guatemalans, and Hondurans have continued to arrive in the United States in large numbers motivated by the war-devastated economies, natural disasters, and the need for family reunification.

Salvadoran family. Photo by Carlos Texca.

SALVADORAN DEMOGRAPHICS IN THE 1990 CENSUS AND THE 2000 CENSUS

The exact numbers of undocumented Salvadorans are not presently available for a variety of reasons. Population statistics from the 1990 Census placed the numbers of Salvadorans in the United States at more than 565,081 people. The 2000 Census originally counted 708,741 Salvadorans living in the United States. But as Census officials made revisions of the original count, the numbers increased significantly as more Salvadorans, as well as other Central Americans, were counted in the review process. Salvadorans presently make up the largest group of Central American people presently living in the United States. Nevertheless, serious questions have been posed on the gathering of these Census statistics as they relate to the Hispanic category, and some of these concerns were specifically addressing the actual undercount of Salvadoran permanent residents and undocumented immigrants and their children born in the United States.

Most immigration scholars and community leaders agree that the decade of the 1990s was a period of increased immigration from Central America, and therefore, the numbers of Central Americans in the 2000 Census were expected to be much higher than those actually reported by the Census Bureau. For example, according to the official Census figures, it appeared that there were at least 100,000 fewer Central and South Americans residing in California in 2000 than there had been in 1990. In California, the numbers are particularly shocking in Los Angeles County, home to the state's most diverse Latino community. A number of Salvadoran and Central American community organizations say the Salvadoran population in Los Angeles at least doubled in the 1990s as a result of increased migration and fertility rates, but the 2000 Census shows that the Salvadoran population declined 26 percent from 253,086 in 1990 to 187,193 in 2000.

Community leaders fear that the Central American communities will be negatively impacted by the lower numbers reported in the Census. Some fear that the undercount might influence the ongoing national debate in Washington, D.C. in regards to the possibilities to grant legal residency to undocumented Salvadoran immigrants. The demographic figures are also used to allocate funding and resources to the communities, and the undercount might mean fewer federal funds available to Central American communities in the future.

Numerous factors must be accounted for when considering the 1990 and 2000 Census undercount of Salvadorans. First, many Salvadorans are undocumented immigrants and do not necessarily like to cooperate with official census enumerators or respond to Census questionnaires. They might be afraid of anyone representing government agencies because of their undocumented immigration status. Second, undocumented persons as well as recently arrived immigrants tend to reside in overcrowded housing conditions, and they are often renters, resulting in less accurate responses to the census questionnaires. Heads of households often declare a lower number of residents in order to ensure that they would not get in trouble with their landlords for having more people living in a housing unit than the number of tenants recorded in the actual rental agreements. Third, the Bureau of the Census has encountered a common practice among immigrants that shows that foreign-born immigrants would declare their own national origin in the questionnaire. But quite often their children would be entered as Americans rather than the national origin or ethnicity of the parents. This practice appears to be common and also skews statistical data on Salvadoran immigrants, especially among those that have recently become naturalized citizens.

In addition, the 2000 Census forms had specific check boxes for Mexican, Cuban, and Puerto Rican. Another blank box was designated "other Hispanic," and that was the place where Salvadorans and other Latin Americans were expected to fill out the information about their national origin. The problem with the form is that it was confusing for many individuals with low literacy rates, and large numbers of people just checked the box and did not write down the information necessary to determine their national origin. Approximately 6.2 million or 17.6 percent of all people who filled out the 2000 Census questionnaires as Hispanics have been in census reports as "other Hispanics" without any specific national origin classification.[2]

A study commissioned by the Population Division of the U.S. Census Bureau and conducted by Census statisticians Arthur R. Cresce and Roberto R. Ramirez investigated the researchers concerns that the format and wording of the Census 2000 question on Hispanic origin may have influenced individuals, and specifically Salvadorans, to provide more generalized responses such as Spanish, Hispanic, or Latino rather than their specific national origins. Cresce and Ramirez examined the individual responses to the place of birth and ancestry questions from people who provided a general response to the question on Hispanic origin. Their study indicates that a substantial proportion of people who provided a general Hispanic response such as "Spanish," "Hispanic," or "Latino" also provided information in the place of birth or ancestry questions about their national origin that was more specific than the information they provided in the question on Hispanic origin. Approximately 5.7 million people chose to respond to the Hispanic category to define their ethnic background during the 2000 Census, and 3.1 million of these individuals also pointed out a specific country of origin in Latin America. Cresce and Ramirez modified the original 2000 Census statistical data if individuals marked they were "Latino" in the question on Hispanic origin and their place of birth was El Salvador; then Salvadoran was used to designate their ethnicity.[3]

After reviewing all the Census questionnaires in question, they found a much higher number of Salvadorans than were actually counted during the Census 2000. Salvadorans experienced a 42.6 percent increase from the simulation (301,999), placing the Salvadoran population at 1,010,740. The total numbers of Central Americans increased from 1,323,830 individuals reported in the 1990 Census to 1,811,676 persons reported in the 2000 Census. After the Cresce and Ramirez count, the number of Central Americans was estimated to be at 2,435,731. It is important to note that the Census Bureau takes the position that the simulated totals presented by Cresce and Ramirez are illustrative and do not replace the official 2000 Census totals for these groups. The totals from the 2000 Census are based on sample estimates from the Spanish/Hispanic/Latino question on the long form and are the official figures.

Another series of important reports on the Hispanic populations characteristics and the Census undercount have been recently published by the Mumford Center for Comparative Urban and Regional Research at the University at Albany, State University of New York. The report on the New Latinos written by John R. Logan, the Center's director, addressed a variety of issues related to the growth and characteristics of the new Latino populations in the United States. The report states that there is a severe underestimate of the new Latinos and introduces a new and improved estimate of the size of these populations. It also presents new evidence that the largest new Latino groups are Dominicans and Salvadorans, both of which doubled in the last decade and have now reached more than 1.1 million. According to the Mumford Center Census count, Central Americans (2,863,063) rank third after Mexicans (23,060,224) and Puerto Ricans (3,640,460) in the Latino population, and Salvadorans (1,117,959) rank fifth in the Latino populations after Mexicans, Puerto Ricans, Cubans (1,315,346), and Dominicans (1,121,257).[4]

The official Census figures as well as other estimates appear to be a low reflection of the actual Salvadoran population numbers, because most of the estimates available through the media, the Salvadoran government, and Salvadoran community organizations put the Salvadoran population at approximately 1.5 million in 1990 and at about 3 million in 2003. (See also Table 2.1.) The

Los Angeles area alone is estimated to have close to a million Salvadorans. The Salvadoran government estimates are also based on the people that have received exit visas for the country as well as those individuals sending monetary remittances to relatives in El Salvador. The Salvadoran government has an accurate count of the numbers of Salvadoran nationals who enter and leave their country. The government database keeps the records of the numbers of Salvadoran permanent residents and tourists who leave their country on their way to the United States. In addition, the Central Bank of El Salvador keeps records on the numbers of persons that send monetary remittances to their relatives in El Salvador.

As previously stated, the Salvadoran immigrants in the United States arrived in the post-1979 migration as permanent residents, asylum seekers, and undocumented immigrants. Scholars and community activists have challenged the demographic figures of the 1990 and the 2000 Census because it is believed that the undercount of the Salvadoran population in the United States is quite significant (Table 4.1). Undocumented workers typically do not fill out the census questionnaires, or they fill out incorrect information due to their fear of being apprehended by INS authorities.

Table 4.1
Salvadoran and Central American Populations in the United States, 1990–2000

	Census 1990	Census 2000	Cresce and Ramirez	Mumford Center
Central Americans	1,323,830	1,811,676	2,435,731	2,863,063
Salvadoran	565,081	708,741	1,010,740	1,117,959
Guatemalan	268,779	407,127	574,785	627,239
Nicaraguan	202,658	194,493	272,655	294,334
Honduran	131,066	131,066	333,636	362,171
Panamanian	92,013	98,475	126,500	164,371
Costa Rican	57,223	71,173	93,583	115,672
Other C.A.	7,000	93,234	23,832	181,228

Source: Arthur R. Cresce and Roberto Ramirez, 2003; Jorge del Pinal, U.S. Bureau of the Census, 1995; Hispanic Population and Residential Segregation Lewis Mumford Center for Comparative Urban and Regional Research University at Albany, State University of New York, http://mumford1.dyndns.org/cen2000/HispanicPop/HspPopData.htm.

SETTLEMENT CHARACTERISTICS OF SALVADORAN POPULATIONS IN THE UNITED STATES

In the 1980s the migration patterns changed because of the sociopolitical and economic conditions prevailing in the Central American region, which resulted in large numbers of Salvadorans and Guatemalans entering the United States without legal documentation or as political asylum applicants. Guatemala and El Salvador have been affected by armed insurgency against the established sociopolitical systems. Since 1980, close to 200,000 people have been assassinated by right-wing paramilitary groups, death squads, and the armed forces in El Salvador and Guatemala.

During this time of war and persecution the most common targets for assassination were labor leaders, Indian leaders, intellectuals, community organizers, Catholic priests, lay preachers, agricultural workers, and students. Most Salvadorans left their country to escape the civil war and to search for personal safety and a new life. Salvadoran society has been severely affected by a long history of political corruption, and the impact of the civil war has been multidimensional. The judicial system does not offer protection to civilians, and threats and intimidation prevent justice and freedom from existing in El Salvador. Many Central American immigrants bring with them those fears and the residual effects of living in a society severely impacted by a climate of terror. They project those fears on to their experiences while living in the United States and are extremely apprehensive of interacting with governmental agencies and the authorities.

According to the 1990 and 2000 Census data, Salvadorans and the U.S.-born children can be found in every state. Salvadorans and Central Americans in general are more likely to reside in the western, northeastern, and southern states than non-Hispanic Whites, and they are less likely to relocate in the Midwest. Salvadorans play an important role in the local economies in their states of residence.

There are important migration currents and networks in the Salvadoran experience in the United States. There is concrete evidence of the existence of at least three different migration patterns that have been followed over time by Central American immigrant populations as they resettle in the United States.

The first pattern is followed by Salvadoran urban dwellers relocating in urban centers in the United States. These individuals lived in San Salvador, Santa Ana, or San Miguel, which are the three largest metropolitan centers in El Salvador. It is expected that individuals who are accustomed to city life will make every possible attempt to relocate in an urban environment to take advantage of the social and economic opportunities available in U.S. cities.

These individuals have higher levels of education and possess some of the skills necessary to be successfully incorporated into the U.S. society. The Central American communities in San Francisco and Los Angeles are examples of this migration. Most Central Americans and specifically Salvadorans reside in the largest U.S. metropolitan areas where they can find ample employment opportunities and better educational opportunities for their children.

The second pattern is observable in rural-origin populations relocating in U.S. urban communities. These populations have lower levels of education and quite often are not well prepared for a successful integration into the U.S. urban environment and the more technically demanding sectors of the labor force. Many of these individuals lack the skills and education to economically succeed and therefore they have become part of an urban underclass in many U.S. metropolitan areas. Central Americans and specifically Salvadorans and Guatemalans are more likely than other Latino groups to work in the service industry. Significant numbers of Salvadorans are employed in the restaurant, hotel, gardening, and domestic sectors of the local economies, particularly in Houston, Washington, D.C., New Jersey, and Long Beach and Los Angeles in California.

Finally, the third pattern is followed by a significant number of Salvadoran rural dwellers relocating in rural areas and continuing to work as agricultural laborers in the United States. This pattern is commonly observed in the large agricultural fields in California, Texas, and Florida. Young Salvadoran men who live in agricultural camps and work as seasonal farm laborers throughout California and the Sun Belt states make up a large segment of this rural population group. Some exceptions to this group are rural people who become entrepreneurs in rural communities in the United States providing services to other Salvadorans and Latinos.

In addition, social class status plays an important role in Salvadorans' relocation and incorporation into the labor force. Immigrants always attempt to relocate in areas where there are ample opportunities for employment based on their own educational and labor skills. One important characteristic of the Salvadoran migrations during the 1980s and 1990s was the fact that many people across different socioeconomic levels arrived in the United States, fleeing the war and political violence. The Salvadoran immigrant population in the United States is heterogeneous, as Salvadorans in the United States come from different socioeconomic and cultural backgrounds, and hold diverse political ideologies. In the 1970s, members of the ruling classes could foresee the developing political crisis, and many of them left El Salvador and resettled in Florida and California. They had already established economic, cultural, and political ties in the United States. Many were educated in American universities, and their socioeconomic status, educational background, bilingual skills, and legal residency status or U.S. citizenship helped them to readily adjust to their new life in this country.

On the other hand, the large numbers of Salvadoran immigrants arriving in the United States after 1979 arrived without legal immigration status and come from middle- and lower-class backgrounds, many of them lacking the economic and social support available to upper-class Salvadorans. A significant number of them do not have the educational, occupational, and language skills needed to succeed in this country. The working class populations throughout the various Central American countries have strong similarities in their social and cultural experiences and have very little in common with the upper class social and cultural experiences.

For example, large numbers of persons from the eastern part of El Salvador relocated in metropolitan centers in the East Coast, Florida, and Texas. This population is mainly rural, or coming from provincial Salvadoran cities and towns. They characteristically have low education levels and very few labor skills that would allow them to succeed in the U.S. urban centers. Many of them have been incorporated into the lowest levels of the U.S. labor force, working as day laborers in construction and landscaping, as domestic workers, and in the hotel and restaurant industries. In Texas, there are large numbers of people from the San Miguel area. In the Washington, D.C. metropolitan area, there are many people from Intipuca, San Miguel, and La Union areas. These populations also have lower levels of educational attainment. The California experience is mixed, but large numbers of urban dwellers and those with more education have relocated in the Los Angeles and San Francisco metropolitan areas. In San Francisco, for example, many people are from San Salvador, Sonsonate, and other major provincial cities.

These new immigrants arrived in the United States as a result of already established ethnic and family networks such as in the case of San Francisco, Los Angeles, Houston, New Jersey, Long Beach, Chicago, New York, and Washington, D.C. Migrations to the United States are a social process that is mediated by long-standing family, friendship, ethnic, home town, and community ties that facilitate moving and ease the immigrant's integration into the new environment. Most Salvadorans are presently residing in California, Texas, New York, Virginia, Maryland, New Jersey, Florida, and Washington, D.C. The largest Salvadoran population in the United States can be found in the Los Angeles Metropolitan area, numbering 312,384. According to the revised 2000 Census figures, almost half of the Salvadoran population in the United States resides in the Los Angeles area, and more than half of the Salvadoran population lives in Southern California.

Community Event at Clínica Romero, Los Angeles. Photo courtesy of Clínica Romero.

Salvadoran community meeting in Houston, TX. Photo by Carlos Texca.

Table 4.2
Salvadoran Population in U.S. Metropolitan Areas Per 1990 and 2000 Censuses

City	2000 Rank	Census 2000	Census 2000 Revision	Mumford 2000	Census 1990	1990 Rank
LA-Long Beach	1	187,193	312,384	340,072	184,513	1
Wash DC-MD-VA-WV	2	85,539	129,631	132,472	51,228	2
Houston, TX	3	50,390	78,325	89,941	39,965	3
Nassau-Suffolk, NY	4	42,500	57,108	61,237	19,143	6
New York, NY	5	28,566	39,662	41,264	27,169	5
San Francisco, CA	6	22,581	37,839	37,948	33,660	4
Dallas, TX	7	19,871	29,073	33,557	10,501	8
Oakland, CA	8	14,002	22,054	25,610	9,901	9
Riverside-San Bernardino	9	11,889	19,524	23,520	8,053	11
Orange County, CA	10	12,122	11,892	19,668	20,607	7
Boston, MA-NH	11	8,450	13,755	19,260	20,341	10
Miami, FL	12	7,339	9,115	13,055	13,179	12
Jersey City, NJ	13	6,570	8,873	13,443	12,737	13
Newark, NJ	14	5,479	8,658	12,012	12,717	16
Las Vegas, NV	15	2,076	7,180	10,704	12,242	20
Chicago, IL	16	6,160	6,802	8,460	10,114	15
Atlanta, GA	17	1,386	6,731	8,883	9,446	24
San Jose, CA	18	6,181	4,975	7,403	9,036	14
Phoenix-Mesa, AZ	19	1,470	2,936	4,720	6,572	25
Fort Lauderdale, FL	20	1,779	3,794	5,771	5,616	22

Source: Hispanic Population and Residential Segregation Lewis Mumford Center for Comparative Urban and Regional Research University at Albany, State University of New York, http://mumford1. dyndns.org/cen2000/HispanicPop/HspPopData.htm.

Again, these statistical figures are based on Census data and might not include a large segment of the undocumented and immigrant population as a result of the Census undercount. Also, according to INS data, the greater majority of undocumented persons in the United States select to migrate to the Southern California region. Therefore, it is possible to say that most undocumented Salvadorans have also migrated to this region. Then the actual numbers of the Salvadoran population must be much higher than the population statistics reflected in the 1990 and the 2000 Census (Tables 4.2 and 4.3).

Table 4.3
Salvadoran Population by Selected States, Per 1990 and 2000 Censuses

State	Census 2000	Census 2000 Revision	Mumford 2000	Census 1990
California	272,999	449,735	493,994	338,769
Texas	79,204	121,399	146,654	58,128
New York	72,713	98,758	105,639	47,350
Virginia	43,653	67,821	68,998	23,537
Maryland	34,433	52,152	55,453	19,122
New Jersey	25,230	35,136	36,091	16,817
Florida	20,701	28,739	30,748	12,400
Massachusetts	15,900	22,416	23,707	9,428
District of Columbia	11,741	18,995	18,969	10,513
Nevada	9,386	14,318	16,131	3,285
North Carolina	8,679	12,390	12,444	1,002
Georgia	8,497	11,500	12,258	1,925
Illinois	7,085	8,884	10,882	6,301
Arizona	3,704	6,037	8,264	2,229
Washington	3,987	6,093	7,562	1,756
Colorado	3,358	5,300	7,024	648
Arkansas	3,471	5,192	6,661	229

(Continued)

**Table 4.3
(continued)**

State	Census 2000	Census 2000 Revision	Mumford 2000	Census 1990
Utah	2,670	4,197	4,417	819
Oregon	2,178	3,772	4,056	849
Minnesota	2,005	3,366	3,431	365
Pennsylvania	1,872	2,452	3,252	1,063
Kansas	1,649	2,778	3,021	348
Connecticut	2,060	3,023	2,860	1,043
Indiana	1,677	2,132	2,818	164
Ohio	1,514	2,192	2,810	685
Tennessee	1,532	2,199	2,742	91
Iowa	1,470	2,301	2,576	337
Louisiana	1,127	2,038	2,465	1,458
Missouri	1,091	1,752	2,161	316
Michigan	1,136	1,365	2,054	501
Rhode Island	1,206	1,450	1,720	902
South Carolina	638	1,029	1,102	146
Wisconsin	671	975	1,168	328
Oklahoma	535	730	1,058	402
New Mexico	514	1,017	2,726	466

Source: Hispanic Population and Residential Segregation Lewis Mumford Center for Comparative Urban and Regional Research University at Albany, State University of New York, http://mumford1.dyndns.org/cen2000/HispanicPop/HspPopData.htm.

CHARACTERISTICS OF CENTRAL AMERICAN IMMIGRANTS IN THE UNITED STATES

According to the 1990 U.S. Census, 1,323,830 Central Americans resided in the United States in 1990. The official 2000 Census figures put the Central American population at 1,811,676 which shows an increase of almost half a million people from the 1990 numbers. The revised numbers by Cresce and Ramirez put the Central American population at 2,435,731, while the Mumford Center has it at 2,863,063. The revised numbers demonstrate an increase of almost 1 million Central Americans living in the United States by the year 2000. According to the official 2000 Census statistical data, the largest group of Central American immigrants continues to be from El Salvador; 565,081 people were reported in 1990 and 708,741 were officially reported in 2000. The revised data by Cresce and Ramirez puts the Salvadoran population at 1,010,740, while the Mumford Center puts it at 1,117,959. The revised numbers show that the Salvadoran population doubled during the 1990s.

The next largest population of Central Americans in the United States are Guatemalans; they began to arrive in large numbers in the United States following the 1954 military coup that overthrew the democratically elected government of Jacobo Arbenz. After the coup, many individuals were exiled or fled the country to escape political persecution; most migrated to California. An urban middle-class population that was made up of intellectuals, political activists, union leaders, and university students characterized this early migration. According to the INS, Guatemala ranks third among the 10 countries that contribute the most to the undocumented immigration to the United States. In U.S. urban centers, most Guatemalans come from urban communities and middle- and working-class backgrounds. They are mostly Spanish-speaking persons with higher levels of education who are more skilled and better prepared to cope in the U.S. culture and society than are the indigenous Mayan people who entered the United States in large numbers in the early 1980s. Nevertheless, Mayans have also settled in large metropolitan centers such as Los Angeles, Houston, and San Francisco.

During the early 1980s, numerous Mayan communities in Guatemala were systematically destroyed as part of a strategic plan of action on the part of the Guatemalan military government. The refugees were subjected to government military actions that massacred the elderly, women, and children who made up the vast majority of the refugee population. Entire populations were involuntarily relocated in strategic areas or were forced to migrate to Mexico or the United States by the repressive campaigns of terror carried out by the armed forces. In rural areas in the Southwest, the Central American population is composed mostly of these indigenous, rural people, most of whom made a living from traditional agriculture in Central America. The Mayan indigenous culture is governed by the rhythm of the corn agriculture and the seasons and people preferred to reestablish their lives in a rural rather than an urban setting. Large numbers of Guatemalan Mayan immigrants are unskilled young males with little education who are employed as seasonal migrant workers on the agricultural farms throughout the sunbelt states. There are numerous Guatemalan Mayans working in the agricultural fields of Florida, Texas, Arizona, Oregon, Washington, and California.

According to the 1990 Census, only about 6,000 Guatemalans resided in the United Sates before 1965. After 1965, the Guatemalan population increased dramatically. The 1990 Census estimated that 268,779 persons of Guatemalan origin lived in the United States; 52,783 were U.S.-born, 215,996 were foreign born. However, in 1995, the INS estimated that there were approximately 121,000 undocumented Guatemalans living in the United States. The official 2000 Census figures puts the Guatemalan population at 407,127 persons, while the revised counts by Cresce and Ramirez estimate 574,785, and the Mumford Center estimates 627,239. It is clear that the Guatemalan population more than doubled during the decade. In addition, the official 2000 Census data counted 93,234, while Cresce and Ramirez estimated 23,832 and the Mumford Center 181,228 persons who classified themselves as "other Central Americans." This category is very complex as it includes a large number of Guatemalan Mayans who do not consider themselves as Guatemalan as well as people from Belize and other ethnic groups within the Central American region.

The Honduran population in 1990 was officially counted at 131,066, and their numbers dramatically increased during the decade. The official 2000 Census counted 237,431 Hondurans, while Cresce and Ramirez estimated 333,636, and the Mumford Center estimated 362,171. The Honduran population more than doubled during the decade and became the third largest Central American national group in the United States. Large numbers of Hondurans came to the United States after the devastation suffered in Honduras by Hurricane Mitch, and many of them were allowed to legally remain in the country by the Nicaraguan Adjustment and Central American Relief Act (NACARA). Most reside on the East Coast, from New York to Florida.

Nicaraguan migrations to the United States began in the early 1930s and were characterized by a flow of people escaping political persecution from the Anastasio Somoza Garcia government. This first wave of Nicaraguans to the United States comprised middle class individuals, professionals, intellectuals, university students, labor organizers, and political dissidents. Many of these Nicaraguan exiles resettled in New York, New Orleans, San Francisco, and Los Angeles. During the 1940s, Nicaraguans entered the United States in search of economic opportunities. Many eventually returned to their country after World War II to become part of a new rising entrepreneurial class.

Salvadoran couple in Hercules, CA. Photo by Carlos Texca.

During the 1960s, the Nicaraguan population in the United States was the largest of the Central American national groups. As the political turmoil in the 1970s escalated to armed conflict, Nicaraguans sought refuge in the United States. After the fall of the Anastasio Somoza Debayle government and the Sandinista victory, many of the original immigrants from the 1930s and 1940s or their descendants returned to live in Nicaragua. During this same period, Nicaraguans associated with the former government began to arrive in the United States as political exiles. Some of the first Nicaraguans to arrive in the United States during the early 1980s were members of the upper class that fled Nicaragua because of their ties with Somoza or their political disagreements with the Sandinista government. Some were businessmen who had economic ties to Somoza, others were former members of the National Guard who escaped from the Sandinista army. Most of these immigrants resettled legally in Florida and California, bringing their wealth and conservative political ideologies with them.

In the mid-80s, most Nicaraguan immigrants to the United States were working class youth escaping from the Contra War and the military draft.

Table 4.4
**Age and Sex of Salvadoran Population in
the United States Per 2000 Census**

Age	Males	Females	Total
Under 21	117,854	108,109	225,963
Over 21	251,102	231,676	482,778
Total	368,956	339,785	708,741

Source: Census 2000 Summary File 4 (SF4).

According to the 1990 Census, 202,658 persons of Nicaraguan origin were residing in the United States, of that total figure 38,363 were U.S.-born, 164,295 were foreign born. In 1995 the INS estimated that there were at least 76,000 undocumented Nicaraguans living in the United States and Nicaragua ranked eighth among the top 10 contributing countries to the undocumented immigration in the United States.

The Nicaraguan American population was 202,658 in 1990, but it showed a slower growth rate than the other Central American groups during the decade as the official 2000 Census count estimated their number at 194,493. Cresce and Ramirez estimated 272,655, and the Mumford Center estimated 294,334.

These groups vary in the ratio of men to women in their U.S. populations; among Salvadorans and Guatemalans, there are more men than women; among the other four groups, there are more women than men. The official 2000 Census estimates a total of 368,956 males and 339,785 females for the Salvadoran population (Table 4.4).

In 1990 the Census Bureau estimated that 57,223 Costa Ricans were in the United States. Of these, 17,785 were U.S.-born and 39,438 foreign born. One can assume that the small number of Costa Ricans in the United States can be attributed to Costa Rica's long history of political stability and democratic tradition. The social, cultural, and political experiences of Costa Ricans, as well as Hondurans, have not been studied in depth.

Compared with other populations, the Central American population in the United States is young, with proportionately more children and fewer elderly. In 1990, the median age of the population was approximately 28 years old. Only 4 percent of the population was 62 years of age or older, and 32 percent were 19 years of age or younger. This youthful age structure is a result of a

Table 4.5
Sex by Age of Salvadoran Population in the
United States Per 2000 Census

Age	Male	Female	Total
Under 12	66,035	62,958	128,993
12–17	28,180	26,934	55,114
18–20	23,639	18,217	41,856
21–24	37,374	28,035	65,409
25–29	49,844	37,810	87,654
30–39	88,796	75,301	164,097
40–49	49,072	50,973	100,045
50–59	17,197	22,005	39,202
60–69	5,530	9,897	15,427
70–79	2,724	5,637	8,361
80–89	753	1,717	2,470
90–99	92	267	359
100–104	20	34	54
Total	368,956	339,785	708,741

Source: Census 2000 Summary File 4 (SF4).

combination of new immigration, which consists mostly of young adults in their reproductive years, and high fertility at younger ages, particularly among the foreign-born. According to the official 2000 Census statistics, 31.3 percent of all males and 31.4 percent of all females are younger than 21 years of age (Table 4.5).

The number of foreign-born persons is significantly larger for every Central American group. Among the Central American population as a whole, the official 1990 Census number of foreign-born persons is 1,046,099, as compared to 277,731 U.S.-born persons. The official numbers of the 2000 Census report the number of foreign-born Salvadorans is 536,162, or 75.3 percent, while only 172,579, or 24.3 percent are U.S.-born (Table 4.6; see also Table 4.3). On the other hand, the Mumford Center reports that 69.6 percent of the Salvadoran population is foreign-born, and 45.9 percent are recent arrivals to the United States. It is important to note that the Mumford

Table 4.6
Salvadoran Population in the United States by
Birthplace and Citizenship Per 2000 Census

	Male	Female	Total
	368,956	339,785	708,741
Native Born:	87,699	84,880	172,579
Born in state of residence in the U.S.	73,772	71,816	145,588
Born in another state in the U.S.	11,987	11,343	23,330
Northeast	2,356	2,018	4,374
Midwest	574	455	1,029
South	4,040	3,615	7,655
West	5,017	5,255	10,272
Born outside the U.S.	1,940	1,721	3,661
Puerto Rico	412	333	745
Born abroad of American parents	1,517	1,388	2,905
U.S. Island Areas	11	0	11
Foreign Born:	281,257	254,905	536,162
Naturalized citizens	59,637	70,352	129,989
Not a citizen	221,620	184,553	406,173

Source: Census 2000 Summary File 4 (SF4).

Center gives an estimate that accounts for a higher number of U.S.-born Salvadorans, and they also have calculated that the Salvadoran population is almost half a million people higher than the official 2000 Census figures.

NOTES

1. Carlos B. Cordova, "Migration and Acculturation Dynamics of Undocumented El Salvadoreans in the San Francisco Bay Area" (PhD dissertation, University of San Francisco, 1986); Carlos B. Cordova, "The Mission District: The Ethnic Diversity of the Latin American Enclave in San Francisco, California," *Journal of La Raza Studies* 2, no. 1 (Summer/Fall 1989): 21–32; Carlos B. Cordova and Jorde del Pinal, *Hispanics-Latinos: Diverse Populations in a Multicultural Society* (Washington, D.C.: National Association of Hispanic Publications, 1996).

2. John R. Logan, *The New Latinos: Who They Are, Where They Are* (Lewis Mumford Center for Comparative Urban and Regional Research, University at Albany, State University of New York, September 10, 2001).

3. Arthur R. Cresce and Roberto R. Ramirez, *Analysis of General Hispanic Responses in Census 2000.* Working Paper No. 72. Population Division. (Washington, D.C.: U.S. Bureau of the Census, 2003).

4. Logan, *The New Latinos.*

PART III

ADJUSTMENT AND ADAPTATION

5

Cultural Baggage and Integration

THE OLD AND THE NEW CULTURES

Salvadoran immigrants in the United States experience a number of cultural and social problems resulting from their lack of understanding of the unfamiliar social and cultural patterns. In addition, many Salvadorans continue to practice many of the social and cultural ways of Salvadoran society that are not necessarily acceptable in the United States. It is seen to be important for the newcomer to become oriented to cultural attitudes, values, and laws of the United States. Time and punctuality are important issues for newly arrived immigrants to understand. In El Salvador, the pace of life is slower and punctuality is not considered as important. It is common for Salvadorans to be very casual about time, as they are often late for appointments, events, and other social functions. But in matters of productivity, Salvadorans are recognized as hard workers, usually work overtime without any complaints, and are considered responsible people who show a minimum level of absenteeism at work.

Recently arrived Salvadorans are not well acquainted with the social rules, etiquette, and expected behavior in their new social and cultural environments, such as scheduling and canceling appointments when not they are able to attend interviews or meetings with agencies, schools, attorneys, doctors, and others. Many of the community agencies providing services to Salvadorans often mention that their Salvadoran clients were regularly late or missed appointments and did not notify the agencies. It is also common to see Salvadorans go to an office without an appointment expecting to be seen by a doctor, attorney, or social worker, making the intake procedures difficult because of the large caseloads serviced by the community agencies or professionals. The new concepts of time and punctuality are the first words of advice given to Salvadoran newcomers by the staff and professionals in various community agencies in the Salvadoran community.

Salvadorans are good conversationalists as they enjoy speaking just about any topic, but particularly Salvadorans love to talk about their job, family, country, and cultural traditions. Salvadorans feel proud about their beaches, typical foods, and other beautiful places in their country. They love funny conversations and giving nicknames to everyone around them. In San Francisco, a woman who had a very short neck was given the name of "head and shoulders"; a man who wears glasses may be called *el choco* ("the blind man"); a person with a flat nose may be called *el chato* or *la chata*; a bald man may be called *pelón* ("bald" or "person with no hair"), or he may be referred to as "Mr. Sunshine" because the sun shines on his head; and a man who has a big mouth and lips might be called *el trompudo* ("the big mouth"). They enjoy telling jokes in any social setting, and it is common practice to tell jokes even during a wake or a funeral, especially with references to funny situations experienced with the deceased person. Americans may have a hard time understanding Salvadoran humor; it is based on topics such as personal defects, sex, and machismo. But most consider that they are only jokes, and this type of humor does not offend most Salvadorans.

Salvadorans are very expressive and demonstrate a range of physical expressions such as kisses, hugs, gestures, and strong handshakes indicating that one is very welcomed. When speaking, Salvadorans generally move their hands, arms, and sometimes their body to emphasize the point of their discussion. Instead of pointing to a subject or direction, Salvadorans tend to make facial gestures. A common one is to pucker the lips in the direction of the person or object one is referring to. This is quite acceptable and is believed to be more polite than pointing one's finger at someone. In addition, eye contact is a very important aspect of interpersonal communication. It is considered an important part of the person's credibility, but an excessive level of eye contact could be perceived as being offensive or intrusive.

Personal encounters between women and men or between women and women usually begin with a kiss on the cheek. The handshakes between them look more like holding hands and may last for a minute or two. Men who are close friends often touch each other on the arm or back, and often greet each other with a firm hug. Salvadorans generally feel comfortable standing or sitting close to each other when talking and touching is often used to emphasize a point in the conversation. Public displays of affection may be acceptable under certain circumstances. Couples may hold hands and

Salvadoran family reception. Photo by Carlos Texca.

kiss each other goodbye. On the other hand, if couples are involved in deep kissing, it is normally not seen as acceptable public behavior.

The way in which people address each other may sound formal. In the Spanish language there are different ways to address people depending on the person's age, position, and relationship to the speaker. The respectful way is the formal *usted* and the friendly, familiar way is *tú* or *vos*. In talking with a superior or with someone who is older, Salvadorans use *usted*. If talking to a colleague or friend, the use of the familiar *vos* is acceptable. Salvadorans generally address people by their last name preceded by the title of *Don, Doña, Señor,* or *Señora* for a married or older person, *Señorita* for a single woman, or by their professional degree. An older woman may also be addressed with the title of *Niña*, which actually means a young girl. A person with a university degree will be addressed as *licenciado/a,* and the term commands respect in all aspects of society, not just the workplace. A high school graduate is addressed as *bachiller.*

It is common to receive invitations to eat at friend's homes, sharing time with their family. Salvadorans love to introduce their families to their friends, and what is better than to join them for dinner at home? They also like to invite friends to participate in family trips on weekends. It is also common practice to not call friends or relatives before going to visit. They simply show up at their friend's door and expect to be entertained. Many of these visits tend to last for hours, and in the United States this practice may not be considered appropriate without previous notice.

FAMILY ISSUES

Salvadoran families, both in El Salvador and in the United States, have dealt with many changes and issues as a result of the experiences they suffered during the Salvadoran war and the involuntary nature of migration of more than 20 percent of the population to the United States. The war had a severe impact on family relations as families were divided because of political affiliations and allegiances. It is well known that just about every Salvadoran family had a relative killed during the war.

As Salvadorans fled the country in search of refuge, families were separated. Sometimes the father would migrate first, and then the mother and children would follow in the journey north a few months, or even years, later. In many

Quinceañera party. Photo by Carlos Texca.

Salvadoran Wedding Reception in Hercules, CA. Photo by Carlos Texca.

cases, the husband and wife left El Salvador, while the children remained to be raised by the grandparents. As time passed and families reunited, many conflicts became apparent as a consequence of the long period of separation. Children often felt abandoned and resented being left behind by one or both parents, and as they reunited the children had grown older and frequently rebelled against the discipline that the parents wanted to impose.

In many instances after the husband and wife were separated for years, once they reunited, the marriage would not work any longer. Sometimes when the husband left first, he found another woman in the United States and had other children with her. This situation would eventually lead to severe problems in the original family structure and relationship.

Most family issues faced by Salvadorans in the United States develop from the differences in values and cultural attitudes held in the mainstream U.S. society and the contrasting nature of the traditional values and culture of El Salvador. For example, children, especially girls, are given more rights and privileges in the mainstream U.S. culture. And when girls reach their teen years and are interested in dating, then further conflicts arise as the Salvadoran and U.S. dating practices for girls are different. When a teenager begins to date in El Salvador, she is frequently required by the parents to have a chaperone present. The chaperone could be a sibling or an older relative or friend. A boyfriend may visit a girl at her home once he has asked for the consent of the parents, but under no circumstances would the boyfriend be allowed to sleep over at the girl's house. The young girl would also not be allowed to sleep over at her boyfriend's home, and they would be expected to abstain from having any sexual relations. On the other hand, boys have more freedom when it comes to dating. In many cases, parents may allow a young man to bring a girlfriend to sleep overnight at their house, but they would not allow their daughters to do the same. Salvadoran parents frequently try to maintain these values and practices in the United States thus creating a great deal of intergenerational and cultural conflicts. As the children grow older and reach marrying age, which is usually in the mid 20s, then they are expected to find a suitable partner who has a similar ethnic background or who is a white American. A great deal of prejudice and discrimination exists when children choose a marriage partner.

In the case of U.S.-born Salvadoran Americans, it is common to see marriages outside the Salvadoran group. It is common for Salvadorans to marry other Central Americans or Latinos. Among those with a long history of family residence in the United States, it is also common to see marriages with individuals outside the Latino ethnicity, and they have married individuals of Irish, Italian, Jewish, African American, or Asian American heritages. Their children are multiracial or multiethnic and present another dimension of ethnic identification. Many of these multiethnic individuals are bilingual in Spanish, English, or other languages also spoken by the marriage partner. Few studies have been done on the particular experiences of this population of Salvadoran Americans.

Other important family issues that affect Salvadoran communities are the values, attitudes, and laws dealing with child rearing practices, corporal punishment, and child abuse. It is common practice in the Salvadoran culture to discipline children by spanking or hitting them with a belt when they misbehave, even in public. What is accepted behavior in El Salvador, however, might be considered child abuse in this country. A high incidence of child abuse by Salvadorans is reported by community agencies, clinics, hospitals, and schools. It is important to familiarize Salvadoran parents with the different values, attitudes, and laws dealing with child rearing to prevent any legal problems for the family. The U.S. child rearing practices are considerably different from the traditional family values and discipline in the Salvadoran society where children are taught respect for the family and their elders. Many Salvadoran immigrants have expressed that this lack of discipline in child rearing practices is the main cause for the changes experienced by the traditional Salvadoran family.

Some Salvadoran men believe that women should not work outside of the house but rather devote their time to raising a family and maintaining the house. Domestic violence is a serious problem and the victims are usually the wives and the children.

Because of the economic pressures and financial needs of Salvadoran families, children are encouraged to find employment and are discouraged from pursuing an education. There is ambivalence about the need for education on the part of the parents, and the family financial needs are considered more important. It is important to note that many Salvadoran parents who migrated from rural communities in El Salvador also have little education. Salvadoran children have a high dropout rate in many parts of the country and often leave school before finishing the eighth grade.

Family conflict is often observed when the wife or the children join the labor force and take part-time jobs to help the family meet their financial demands. Women tend to find employment faster than men, even though the jobs may demand long hours, entail abusive treatment, and pay low wages. Depression, alcoholism, and emotional and self-esteem problems tend to develop in the father or head of household, because it goes against the traditional image of

Children's Piñata Party. Photo by Carlos Texca.

Salvadoran teens in Daly City, CA. Photo by Carlos Texca.

the father as the provider of the family, especially if the father is unemployed at the time.

Salvadoran American children frequently become the repositories of their parents anxieties, ambitions, dreams, needs, and conflicts because of the social and economic pressures. Children are given many adult responsibilities that are not expected for children at their stage of psychosocial development in the U.S. society. Children become the liaisons between the parents and the mainstream society. Children are used as guides and interpreters for the elders in the family while assuming more responsibilities. It is common for children to be taken away from school by the parents to assist them with their interactions with attorneys, doctors, or with the mainstream in general. The children become the family translators and interpreters, while the older children help take care of their younger siblings and assume more adult responsibilities than general society would expect. These situations create resentment and a feeling of entrapment in children, and they sometimes develop depression and dissatisfaction with the family. As a result, many children find a sense of family and support system in the gang lifestyle and culture, instead.

Another issue affecting Salvadoran American families is that the young usually acculturate faster than the older adults. Children and teenagers may also adopt the values and attitudes of the U.S. society and might prefer them over the traditional Salvadoran cultural values. These situations create conflict, frustration, and division in the family structure.

THE ADJUSTMENT AND CULTURAL ADAPTATION OF SALVADORAN IMMIGRANTS

The processes of acculturation and assimilation have a wide variety of meanings depending on the disciplinary framework used in the analysis of the immigrant experience. A working definition of acculturation will be used in this book based on the framework of cultural pluralism that emphasizes the fact that immigrants and their children in a new society are able to retain their original cultural identity while learning to interact and adequately function in the mainstream society. Cultural pluralism has its foundations on the notion that there will be a significant level of tolerance and acceptance of others on the part of the mainstream population. In addition, the minority groups, immigrants, or other ethnic groups will have the willingness to learn the rules of the new cultural and social systems. These processes of learning the new cultural and social experiences may be referred to as acculturation.

Furthermore, acculturation involves a series of dynamic processes in which the adult immigrant acquires the basic survival skills of the new society, such as learning a new language, finding employment, and securing housing, as well as the survival skills within other existing ethnic communities. Language acquisition is an important measure and determinant of acculturation, because language is a primary element of culture, and it is the dynamic principle of enculturation or the learning of culture by children.[1] Acculturation will be herein meant to describe and analyze the dynamics of interaction between Salvadoran populations and the U.S. society. Included in this definition are the intra-ethnic, inter-ethnic, and minority-majority relations within the U.S. society.

The process of assimilation on the other hand, may be described as the total absorption of the individual by the new society. Under this form of majority-minority relations, the original cultural patterns and traditions are abandoned while those of the new society are adopted in its totality. For Latin Americans, acculturation in a pluralistic society is the most acceptable process, allowing for mutual borrowing of cultural traits without abandoning their original culture and personality structure. Acculturation allows the individual to be bilingual and bicultural; it enriches the individual's experience and permits proper functioning and interaction in the mainstream society and culture.

Upon their initial arrival in the United States, Salvadoran immigrants frequently experience "culture shock," a condition that is manifested through a sense of anxious disorientation. Most immigrants experience culture shock right after finding themselves in a new and substantially different way of life, where they are forced to interact in a new social and cultural environment where a different language is spoken. New immigrants find themselves in a situation that includes a general unfamiliarity with the customs and expectations of the new country and engage themselves in a marginal level of interaction with the mainstream society and culture. Like most newcomers to the United States, Salvadoran immigrants have a lack of understanding of the societal rules and cultural patterns, which in turn, makes them feel inadequate and alienated.

Whenever the new environment and society are more difficult and hostile toward the immigrant, the immigrant will suffer more in the acculturation process. In the case of undocumented Salvadorans in the United States, the added pressures of their immigration status and the lack of U.S. governmental support make their acculturation processes much more difficult. Undocumented Salvadorans have additional stresses in their social adaptation experiences because of fears of apprehension and deportation by immigration officials. Many undocumented Salvadorans who arrived in the United States during the civil war in the 1980s suffered from mental health problems, which in many cases may have been aggravated by the forced nature of their relocation.

The stresses created by forced relocation may have physiological, psychological and socio-cultural causes. During the 1980s and 1990s, Salvadorans suffered a variety of physiological stresses created by the civil war and their involuntary migration experiences. Individuals suffered from a variety of tropical diseases such as parasites, gastroenteritis, malnutrition, and tuberculosis, as well as increased mortality rates. Psychological stresses common in political refugees were also manifested in Salvadoran immigrants throughout the United States. They suffered from post-traumatic stress disorders (PTSD) associated with the environment of violence and the effects of the civil war in El Salvador. These individuals were reported to suffer anxiety and acute depression, which in many occasions resulted in hospitalization and intensive psychiatric treatment.

Undocumented Salvadorans also suffer the sociocultural stress related to the economic, political, and cultural effects of their migration. Besides losing all their personal possessions during the move, forced migrants may find hard-earned skills of little immediate utility in making a living in the new environment. Economic migrants may find themselves in similar situations. Another important form of stress is brought on by a major reduction in their Salvadoran cultural experiences due to a temporary or permanent loss of behavioral patterns, economic practices, institutions, and symbols. This affects all immigrants, both forced and voluntary.

OBSTACLES TO CULTURAL ADAPTATION AND SOCIAL INTEGRATION

The most common recurring acculturation problems faced by Central American and, specifically, Salvadoran immigrants include language acquisition; lack of employment opportunities, labor market exploitation, and low income; educational attainment; health care and mental health care access; and cultural differences. For those living in the United States without immigration documents, their "undocumented" status is the most overwhelming problem. Undocumented Central American immigrants have more difficulties in adapting to their host society than do their legal counterparts. Their undocumented immigration status, constant fear of deportation by immigration officials and, often, psychological problems caused by the repressive political conditions in which they previously lived in Central America affect their daily lives and resettlement experiences. Many undocumented Central Americans feel trapped because they are not able to return to their homeland because of their documentation status and their fear of persecution and lack of personal safety. They encounter a series of difficulties that prevent them from becoming fully incorporated into U.S. society and culture.

Language Acquisition

Language acquisition is considered an important priority in the acculturation process. Mastering the English language is necessary to improve the socioeconomic and cultural experience of recently arrived immigrants. The higher the degree of proficiency in the new language, the greater the opportunities and skills the individual will possess to enable him/her to effectively interact in the mainstream society.

Individuals with professional degrees or some formal education demonstrate higher level language acquisition than do those who are unskilled laborers; this facilitates labor market opportunities. However, for those individuals who do not have legal status in the United States, it is very difficult to find work in their fields. Central American professionals, university professors, and teachers encounter serious obstacles because they cannot find employment in their areas of expertise. Many professionals experience downward social mobility. Many

Central American students at San Francisco State University. Photo by Carlos Texca.

are employed in occupations where they cannot use their training or skills; this generates frustration and emotional and psychological problems. Further, their high expectations for opportunities available in the United States, and the disappointment in not fulfilling their expectations creates a high degree of stress.

Age also plays an important role in the acquisition of language skills. Younger individuals demonstrate higher motivation to learn English than do older persons. With the exception of those with a professional background, middle-age and adult-age immigrants often limit their social interaction to their ethnic enclave and demonstrate a preference of retaining Spanish as their primary means of communication. This provides them with social comfort but constrains their integration into the labor market, American culture, and society.

Although all Central American immigrants are confronted by cultural differences when they resettle in the United States, Central American indigenous people face particular challenges in their adaptation to the United States. Many indigenous people speak neither English nor Spanish; many have never lived outside their rural villages; many have lived their entire lives working in the seasonal cycle of agriculture. The situation of Guatemalan Mayans who have settled in the state of Florida serves as an example. Most Guatemalan Mayans working in Florida are Kanjobal-speaking people from the town of San Miguel Acatlan located in the northern province of Huehuetenango.

Their adjustment has been difficult because they are mostly monolingual, speaking only Mayan languages, and hold non-Western cultural values. Mayans in Florida have encountered cultural problems that disrupt their culture and religion and force the discontinuation of their rituals and cultural traditions. The Mayan refugees in Florida work in the citrus fields and are no longer engaged in the cycle of corn agriculture.

Educational Issues

Salvadorans in California tend to be long-term residents who are generally better educated than immigrants from Mexico. Two-thirds of California's Salvadoran population have been living in the state for more than 14 years, and a significant number were professionals who fled the Salvadoran civil war. According to data from the 2000 Census, about one-fourth of the Salvadoran immigrants older than 25 years of age have attended college, a figure that is about twice the number of Mexican immigrants. That high level of educational attainment may contribute to the fact that 25 percent of Salvadoran American families headed by one or more Salvadoran immigrants earn more than $50,000 a year. But it is important to note that more than half of the Salvadoran population has salaries of less than $30,000 per year. This population of low earners continues to exist despite the fact that 81 percent of Salvadoran men are steadily employed, a figure that is much higher than the 61 percent of U.S.-born Latino men.[2]

Latino adults in the United States have a significant disadvantage in educational attainment in relation to other population groups. However, there are significant differences between Latino subgroups, and the contrasting educational profiles of Central Americans exemplify some of these differences. As noted, compared with other Latin Americans, Central Americans have lower rates of educational attainment. Also noted is that there are significant differences in rates of educational attainment between naturalized and noncitizen immigrant populations, with citizen populations having much higher rates of educational attainment.

It is noteworthy that Central American students lead the statistics in high school drop out rates in various parts of the country. Their education and cultural heritage are at risk. These students are affected by a wide range of socioeconomic, cultural, political, and demographic factors such as area of residence, degree of community support, length of residence in the United States, and individual levels of cultural adaptation and social integration.

Poverty appears to play a significant role in educational attainment among youth. Among Latinos generally, the high school dropout rate has ranged from two to three times the rate of other children depending on the measure that was used. Poverty forces teenagers prematurely into the labor force, and problems of overcrowded, poorly equipped big-city schools, which most Salvadorans attend, also boost dropout rates and discourage education. Central Americans also suffer from discrimination in U.S. schools and in their communities. One glaring obstacle to educational attainment in higher education is lack of documentation status. Almost all institutions of higher learning require access to a social security number and other evidence of legal immigration status. Legislation, such as Proposition 187 in California, was designed to limit the educational opportunities of undocumented persons even further.

Employment Issues

Employment opportunities are considered one of the major issues influencing the social adaptation and economic stability of Salvadorans in this country. The available employment opportunities are dependent on the immigration status. The economic opportunities available to undocumented Salvadoran workers in the mainstream society are extremely limited; employment is often found only in factories, construction and janitorial firms, the hotel and restaurant industry, or in domestic services where English proficiency may not be required. Individuals with higher levels of education or English communication skills may be able to find better paid employment.

On the other hand, many undocumented Salvadorans or those with less education end up working within the enclave economy where they find employment for sub-minimum wages and are subjected to abuse and exploitation. Working conditions in the enclave appear to be acceptable, mainly because wages are often paid in cash. Cash payments minimize the fears of disclosing an individual's undocumented status to strangers and do not require showing the proper documentation needed to work such as a social security number or an alien registration card. Many need to hold more than one full-time job to meet their financial needs, forcing these immigrants to take whatever employment is available for them.

Professionals, university professors, and teachers encounter serious obstacles because they cannot find employment in their specific areas of expertise. Many professionals have experienced downward social mobility and are often employed in menial occupations that generate emotional and psychological problems. It is difficult for attorneys, doctors, architects, or professors to earn a living as dishwashers, janitors, or baby sitters. Their high expectations regarding the opportunities available in the United States, and the disappointment of not being able to fulfill them, creates a high degree of stress.

THE STRUCTURE OF SALVADORAN AMERICAN COMMUNITIES

The Central American population in the United States includes people who trace their family's resettlement in the United States to the 1800s, as well as those who have recently arrived. It includes people who have all the privileges of citizenship, as well as those who fear government detection and are most vulnerable to discrimination, exploitation, and violation of basic rights. It includes both urban and rural people. It includes people whose primary language is Spanish; people whose primary language is an indigenous Indian language such as Quiché, Kanjobal, or Miskitu; and people whose primary language is English. It includes people who wish to stay in the United States as well as those who dream of returning to live in their homelands. It includes people of all races, many ethnicities, and very diverse socioeconomic backgrounds. It includes people who have been incorporated into American society in very different ways; some welcomed as workers or refugees, others rejected. These millions of people who trace their ancestry to countries in Central America have had an important impact on the social, cultural, economic, and political fabric of the United States and will continue to do so in the future.

Since the early 1980s, large numbers of Salvadorans have traveled north to the United States and Canada. In the United States, Salvadorans usually resettle in communities where other Salvadorans or Central Americans have already established a cultural and economic base, because newly arrived immigrants prefer to relocate in places that look familiar and remind them of their home. Newcomers attempt to move the shortest distance not only in space, as they like to remain in contact with a familiar environment, but also in terms of the psychological and sociocultural context of their lives.[3] Salvadoran immigrants and refugees have created ethnic enclaves in San Francisco, Los Angeles, Washington, D.C., New York, Houston, and other cities in the United States as the means of creating familiar social environments, support systems, and survival strategies.

Different levels of organizing have taken place over many decades in Salvadoran communities in this country. Communities are diverse as a result of a long history of migration of Salvadorans to the United States. Salvadorans have settled in San Francisco and Los Angeles since the late 1800s while other communities were established later; therefore, the Salvadoran American communities are not made up by a homogeneous population. Individuals may be immigrants or 1st, 2nd, 3rd, or 4th generation born in the United States. They have acculturated and adapted to the U.S. society at different levels. Some persons may discriminate against recent immigrants because of their lack of

English-language proficiency and acculturation. Recent immigrants may be prejudiced against those with a long period of residence in the United States or those who are U.S.-born, based on their lack of proficiency in the Spanish language and their lack of understanding and competency of the Salvadoran cultural experience.

Central Americans have arrived in the U.S. metropolitan centers following already established social migration networks. These networks are an essential mechanism in the migration patterns and cultural adaptation dynamics of Central Americans in the United States. Social migration networks provide the new immigrants with a series of support structures that help them relocate and adapt to their new social environment in the United States. These social migration networks may be organized according to:

1. Family ties that could be either nuclear or extended. Most likely for Salvadorans and other Central Americans the extended family plays a very influential role in deciding to migrate as well as in helping the immigrants adjust and adapt to their new home in the United States.
2. Neighborhood networks in which friends and acquaintances who are already established in the host society may help the new immigrants relocate and adapt in the U.S. society.
3. Town or village networks, in which people from the same town help others migrate and adjust in the United States.
4. Ethnic or national networks, in which people of the same ethnicity or national origin help others of migrate, adjust, and adapt in the United States.

Ethnic networks provide a sense of security and belonging for immigrants. They need to find in the host country the traditional social and cultural experiences that were present in their original country and that provided them with psychological satisfaction and security, so they can move with confidence toward interaction with the new, larger society.[4]

Newly arrived Salvadorans relocate in Latino ethnic enclaves as a response to discrimination and their lack of understanding of the new societal systems that they encounter in the United States and usually limit their primary relationships to members of their own national or ethnic group. Furthermore, this phenomenon is encouraged by the immigration status of undocumented Salvadorans, which prevents them from fully interacting with the mainstream society and culture, creating at the same time fear of persecution, insecurity, and a variety of mental health problems. Salvadoran immigrants prefer to interact with individuals of their own culture and nationality to gradually adapt to the new social environment.

As the new immigrants establish themselves in the ethnic enclave, most of their primary relationships and institutions are maintained almost exclusively within the intra-ethnic dimension. Because Salvadorans generally relocate in United States cities where there is already a significant number of Salvadorans or Central Americans; their social and cultural interaction is usually limited to the Salvadoran or Central American experiences found in the ethnic community.

It is quite common for Salvadorans to help other family members or friends relocate, and the already established immigrants help the newcomers adjust to their new life in the United States. People involved in the social migration networks can help with the logistics of the trip from El Salvador to the United States by providing the prospective immigrant with the legal sponsorship to become lawful permanent residents, or by providing monetary and logistic help for the journey north. For those coming to the United States with undocumented immigration status, people in the United States or at home may help defray the cost of the journey as well as the cost of the smuggler or "coyote" who will help to cross the U.S. border and then bring the immigrants to their new home. Established enterprises in El Salvador provide transportation and border crossing services that may cost anywhere from $5,000–20,000. Many family members lend money to relatives so that they can move to the United States, and the loans must be repaid once the new immigrant finds employment.

In addition, friends or relatives may give temporary room and board to recent arrivals until they can become independent, which may take from a few months to a few years, depending on the new immigrant's economic resources, educational background, occupational skills, and English-language proficiency. The new arrivals use their ethnic or family contacts to secure employment, housing, or to meet any of their immediate needs. Individuals already established in the network provide the newcomers with information and a basic orientation. The new arrivals are also provided with information and leads regarding employment opportunities. In many instances, employment opportunities—mostly low-paying jobs available for newcomers or undocumented workers—have been secured for them by their family members or friends.

Once the new immigrants settle down, get adjusted to their new social environment, and are able to save enough money, they begin to look for independent housing and better economic opportunities. They may also begin to help other relatives back in El Salvador make the journey north to join them in their new life. After a few years of living in the Latin American neighborhoods, many Central American immigrants socially adapt to the U.S. lifestyle. They acquire the necessary employment and language skills as well as the necessary education to fully participate in the mainstream economic life, and they may relocate in other ethnically mixed neighborhoods or suburban communities. Others take advantage of economic opportunities and develop business enterprises in the Latin American neighborhoods and utilize the immigrant labor force to maximize their profits.

One of the important features of the Salvadoran migration experience is the role of *remesas,* monetary remittances, that are sent back to family members in El Salvador. The remittances play an important role because they are helping maintain the Salvadoran economy that has been struggling for many decades. The money sent from the United States back to El Salvador is the largest source of income in the local economy in El Salvador. Salvadoran official sources state that about $2 billion dollars enter the country annually in the form of monetary remittances sent to family members by Salvadoran immigrants. This is more than El Salvador makes from its other most important source of revenue, coffee. Many towns and villages in El Salvador are able to survive the economic crisis facing the country thanks to the *remesas* flowing in from the United States.

The Central American enclaves in San Francisco, Los Angeles, New Jersey, New York, Washington, D.C., Boston, and Houston among others, demonstrate a well-diversified economic base and division of labor. There are also emerging Salvadoran communities in Las Vegas, Nevada; Greensboro and Raleigh in North Carolina; and in Atlanta, Georgia. The economic structure of the enclave provides for availability of bilingual professional services to the community. The ethnic enclave allows the immigrant to receive legal, educational, immigration, medical, dental, accounting, income tax consulting, counseling, employment training and referrals, food services, and others. This sector is made up not only of immigrants, but first and second generation Central Americans and other Latin Americans providing professional services. Other bilingual ethnic and mainstream professionals and merchants also provide services in Spanish within the enclave.

The enclave provides familiar settings by allowing the development of regional or hometown associations that support the immigrant with cultural, social, and recreational activities. Regional associations and the enclave provide new immigrants with the support structures and resources that develop cultural identification, security, and a sense of belonging in the host society. Regional associations allow the preservation of cultural traditions and the retention of a strong cultural and national identification as a Salvadoran and a Central American. Many regional associations are named after towns, cities, states, or regions where the immigrant populations originate in Central America. Some organizations are affiliated with Central American religious societies, sports clubs, artistic or cultural organizations, or social service organizations. Some of the most popular regional associations are identified with soccer or baseball clubs that participate in Latin American or mainstream sports leagues. These associations are well organized and have large memberships. Their members pay dues and usually rent a small place as a recreation center. A number of soccer and baseball clubs organized by members of the Salvadoran community create numerous opportunities for the local youth. For instance, a midnight soccer league sponsored by the city and county of San Francisco is run by Salvadorans and targets youths associated with the local gangs. This has proven to be a successful option to prevent youth gangs and violence in the Latino community.

Some of the most active and better organized home town associations include those on the East Coast that are associated with the Salvadoran towns of Intipuca and Chirilagua and Santa Elena in Los Angeles and San Francisco. These associations organize regular events that include picnics, dances, an annual ball, and other fundraisers for their hometown communities in El Salvador. In the San Francisco Bay Area, there are other groups that are informally organized such as the Sonsonate Association. This association is composed of immigrants that arrived in the Bay Area in the 1950s and 1960s. They come from middle-class origins and hold conservative political orientations. Many of them are U.S. citizens and members of the Republican Party. Their activities are merely social, and most of them do not participate in political activities for the local Salvadoran community but are individual members of the Hispanic chamber of commerce and other associations that promote economic growth for their business affairs.

Ethnic enclaves develop as sub-groups within society as a result of an antagonistic social environment where the members of the immigrant or minority group are not totally functional in the mainstream society and thus become victims of discrimination and economic exploitation. Therefore, the Salvadoran community is where the primary relationships are. As they involve intimacy and privacy, primary relationships are restricted mostly to members of the same national or ethnic group. On the other hand, their interaction in the mainstream society is often limited to their job, as it represents the individual's public life or the pursuance of secondary relationships for utilitarian and survival reasons. The immigrants only develop secondary relationships at the societal level because that is the place where they experience discrimination as a result of racial, cultural, and linguistic differences.

As can be seen in the Salvadoran American communities, they have limited political power. The Central American immigrant communities are divided on issues related to national identity and origin, political affiliations in Central America and the United States, ethnicity, and socioeconomic status. These divisions do not currently allow the necessary social cohesion needed to transform this population into a strong political body that will be able to seek viable political solutions to the problems and realities that they encounter in this society. It has been seen that there is a need to develop responsible and accountable political and social activists within the Salvadoran American community so as to critically affront the wide range of problems that they face.

Salvadorans in the United States are greatly interested in keeping up with the news and current events in El Salvador. However, there is considerable variation in the ways in which they attempt to keep informed. Some read Salvadoran newspapers, which are more readily available than other Central American newspapers, largely as a result of the Salvadoran community being larger and more "established," hence, more cohesive.

More men than women read the newspapers from the home country, as it is most likely the women are busy doing household chores when they are not working, while men have more leisure time to read. Most Salvadorans keep informed through television and radio news programs. In the cases of both newspapers and radio/television, most Salvadoran immigrants receive their news about El Salvador through Spanish language media. Another important source of news from home is contact with family members, particularly by phone.[5]

THE EMERGENCE OF POLITICAL ORGANIZING IN CENTRAL AMERICAN COMMUNITIES IN THE UNITED STATES

The sociopolitical characteristics of the Central American immigrant populations and, specifically, Salvadoran American immigrant populations are diverse. The Salvadoran community in San Francisco has had difficulties in becoming a cohesive and empowered group in the San Francisco political and social arenas as a result of various social and political factors, which tend to divide the various Salvadoran groups.

The Salvadoran communities have divergent political ideologies ranging from conservative right-wing views to orthodox Marxist orientations based on the political ideologies and affiliations held in El Salvador. Individuals living in the United States may be sympathizers with political parties in El Salvador,

Anti-CAFTA demonstration in front of Salvadoran consulate in San Francisco, CA. Photo by Jorge Castillo.

which may include ARENA, Partido de Conciliación Nacional (PCN), or the FMLN. Their affiliations also reflect their political philosophy or ideology. In addition, Salvadoran Americans are also politically diverse when observing their affiliations in the U.S. political parties, as there are Salvadorans registered and actively involved in the Democratic, Republican, and other independent political parties.

In many ways, political diversity and especially political extremism in Central American communities has constrained the development of social cohesion and political empowerment for all of its members. To date, Salvadoran American communities have not unified around issues associated with their shared Salvadoran national identity, regionalism, political party affiliations, ethnicity, religion, and/or socioeconomic status.

One major drawback to political empowerment in many communities has been the common belief on the part of the immigrants that their residence in the United States will be temporary. Consequently, many Salvadorans remain isolated and neglect to participate in domestic political affairs at the community, municipal, state, or national levels. Unless an individual has some degree of political sophistication or experience, most Salvadoran Americans show signs of apathy toward U.S. political and social issues. Over the years, community activists have attempted to persuade Central American immigrants to become U.S. citizens and to participate in the electoral process. Until recently, these efforts were fruitless because many Central Americans believed that if they became U.S. citizens they would betray their national identity and citizenship. The situation changed rapidly in the 1990s because of the anti-immigrant currents affecting the United States, the passage of Proposition 187 in California in 1995, the passage of the Welfare Reform Bill in 1996, and new immigration legislation initiated by the Federal government. These changes motivated thousands of Central Americans to apply for U.S. citizenship to retain their social service benefits and protect themselves from INS harassment. For the first time in decades, community activism and political empowerment began to take root in Central American communities throughout the country.

Within the Central American population, the undocumented status of the population has contributed to the community's difficulty in achieving formal political power. However, many Central American community organizations have attempted to achieve political power by forming organizations that are closely associated with political parties or organizations in their home country or region. For example, Casa El Salvador, Casa Nicaragua, and some Guatemalan organizations have close ties with Central American Leftist revolutionary movements. In California, these groups successfully used solidarity

CARECEN office in Washington, D.C. Photo by Carlos Texca.

actions against U.S. policies in Central America. Their success was based on the fact that they did not limit their activities to organizing only with Latin American communities. They reached out to the mainstream and created multiethnic coalitions, working closely with international solidarity coalitions and networks such as the Committee in Solidarity with the people of El Salvador (CISPES), Amnesty International, and the Emergency Response Network. Their main objective was to deal with issues that directly affected the Central American region, but they did not place their main emphasis on the empowerment efforts within the local communities.

Organizations such as the Coalition for Immigrant and Refugee Rights and Services work within a local community structure to advocate for immigrant issues, especially for abuses against immigrant women. Their efforts have been successful in organizing within the local immigrant community by creating bridges between different immigrant communities. Central American service organizations have been particularly effective in the internal affairs of the Central American community while, at the same time, they represent the refugees in the mainstream society and local political structures. Some of these organizations are the Comité de Refugiados Centro Americanos (CRECE)

Salvadoran community activists meeting for a national meeting in Washington, D.C. Photo by Carlos Texca.

which provides refugees with social services; the Central American Resource Center (CARECEN) which provides legal representation for refugees in immigration hearings, health referral services, training for health promoters, a youth tattoo removal program, and literature; and El Rescate and Clínica Romero in Los Angeles, which provides a wide range of services. During the mid-1980s and the early-1990s, CARECEN played an important role in the formation of the Central American National Network (CARNET*)*, which included 38 refugee agencies and grassroots organizations in the United States. The development of local leadership is an important priority in the selection and training of low-income Central American immigrants who work as immigrant and refugee rights promoters and advocates. The promoters provide services to the immigrant community, speak in public forums, and monitor and attempt to impact legislation affecting the Central American immigrant community at the municipal, state, and national levels.

In these organizations, immigrants work together to empower other immigrants. Because of their organizational structure, history, philosophy, and their empowerment efforts, these community groups are recognized to represent the leadership in the Central American refugee and immigrant community. These organizations work closely with the religious organizations, network of churches, Catholic Charities, Baptist Ministries, and the Quakers, among others. They receive funds and direct services from religious organizations and private foundations. One successful model is St. Peter's Church in San Francisco's Mission District. Refugees working side by side with the local pastor have created a Central American refugee program that provides a wide variety of services such as a long-term shelter for homeless men, mental health counseling, rights advocacy, day laborer advocacy, cultural support, and language classes to the local Mayan population.

RELIGIOUS ISSUES AFFECTING CENTRAL AMERICAN COMMUNITIES IN THE UNITED STATES

Recent Latin American immigrants often feel alienated from the Catholic religious practices in the United States. This feeling may result from the cultural differences in ritual practices, the physical appearance and architectural design of the Church buildings, the lack of faith in the cult of the saints, and the small number of Latino priests in the United States. The Catholic Church has continued to try to analyze the reasons why Latino immigrants are converting from Catholicism to Protestantism. Central American immigrants and specifically Salvadorans have expressed a high degree of dissatisfaction with

U.S. Catholicism. The lower the levels of acculturation to the U.S. culture, the higher the levels of dissatisfaction this population demonstrates. Many Central American immigrants will say that they converted to Protestantism because Protestant churches provide a feeling of family and community, and they are sensitive and understanding to the immigrant's cultural experiences.[6]

Protestant ministers have taken their role as missionaries seriously by actively walking and targeting Latino and Central American neighborhoods. They place a high degree of importance on their work among the immigrant youth, by taking on challenging issues such as drug abuse, gang violence, and education. In most cases, these ministers who are recruited from the ranks of the local populations, are fluent in Spanish and are competent in the immigrant's cultural experience.[7]

Latino immigrants also believe that the U.S. Catholic Church does not provide an adequate level of training in the faith and the teachings of the Bible, whereas the Protestant churches place a great deal of importance on these areas. A significant number of recent Central American immigrants worked closely with and were active participants in the "Church of the Poor" and Liberation Theology in their home countries. Liberation Theology emphasizes the critical analysis of the scriptures and their direct applications to the family, the community, and society at large. Liberation Theology states that the relationship between humans and God is horizontal and extends outward from self to others, which is different from that of the Catholic hierarchy.

The popular church in Central America took a radical approach by incorporating the traditional culture and the socioeconomic realities of most of the population into their rituals. Culture was expressed through the Mass, which included the musical element of guitars and songs that represented cultural traditions and criticisms of the political and socioeconomic realities of Central America. Many priests also incorporated murals into their church buildings that represented historical scenes or themes associated with the liberation of the poor from the oppression of the rich and the military. The Catholic Church has demonstrated a high level of commitment and support for the poor and the oppressed in Central America since the 1970s, and when Central American immigrants arrive in the United States they have a high level of expectations from the Catholic Church and its hierarchy.

U.S. Catholicism stresses guidance in personal life and in understanding the faith. Latin American Catholics are also looking for spiritual growth while attempting to understand the rituals and religion. The problem arises with the nature of U.S. Catholicism in the sense that it may be too complex for recent immigrants to understand.

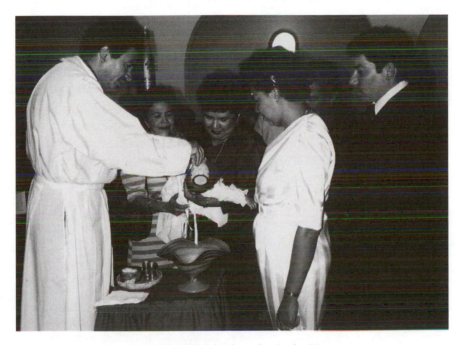

Salvadoran family baptizing their child. Photo by Carlos Texca.

The religious practices of Central American Catholicism are quite different from those in the United States. The popular religion in Central America combines the religious experiences brought to the region by the Catholic missionaries during the sixteenth century as they blended with the native indigenous religious structure, tradition, and ritual practice through 500 years of colonization. The religious rituals and traditions of Central Americans include a strong devotion to the Catholic Saints who in numerous instances are syncretized with the indigenous deities. The ritual traditions are dynamic and vibrant. They involve the community in worship and personal and collective religious activities that include baptism, fiestas, offerings, processions, penance, and more.

The Catholic Church has traditionally provided services to underserved populations and still has yet to develop a critical awareness of the reality of Central American immigrants in the United States. Some see that the Catholic Church must continue in a position of advocacy providing legal and survival services through the office of Catholic Charities. The Central American community in San Francisco had an interesting reaction when the Catholic Social Services changed its name to Catholic Charities. Many immigrants refused to seek help because of negative associations with the term charities. Central

Americans are proud people and will first exhaust all possible avenues for self-help before seeking "charity" from the Church. Others think that there is a contradiction in the name when the Church charges for legal services if they are "charity." In Central America the support systems originate in the family, and the programs that are considered as social services in the United States are almost unknown in Central America. Charity is provided by the government, the Church, and benevolent associations, and only in extreme cases to individuals who cannot provide for themselves. The common attitude is that if a person is physically able and can work, then one must provide for oneself without expecting society to provide support.

NOTES

1. A.M. Padilla, "The Role of Cultural Awareness and Ethnic Loyalty in Acculturation, in *Acculturation: Theory, Models and Some New Findings,* ed. A.M. Padilla (Boulder, Colo.: Westview Press, 1980).

2. David Hayes-Bautista, "UCLA's Center for the Study of Latino Health and Culture," report in "Study Compares 2 Latino Groups' Education Levels," by Patrick McDonnell, *Los Angeles Times,* February 24, 2004. http://www.cesla.med.ucla.edu/html/salvarticle.htm.

3. T. Scudderand E. Colson, "From Welfare to Development: A Conceptual Framework for the Analysis of Dislocated People, in *Involuntary Migration and Resettlement: The Problems and Responses of Dislocated People,* ed. A. Hansen and A. Oliver-Smith (Boulder, Colo.: Westview Press, 1982).

4. J.P. Fitzpatrick, J.P., "The Importance of 'Community' in the Process of Immigrant Assimilation, *International Migration Review* I, no. 1 (Spring 1966): 5–16.

5. Based on a study done by Carlos B. Cordova and Susanne Jonas on Salvadoran and Guatemalan Transnational experiences. Project funded by the North South Center, University of Miami.

6. Gerardo Marin and Raymond Gamba, "Expectations and Experiences of Hispanic Catholics and Converts to Protestant Churches" (San Francisco: University of San Francisco, Social Psychology Laboratory, *Hispanic Studies,* February 1990).

7. A.F. Deck, "Fundamentalism and the Hispanic Catholic," America, January 25, 1985.

6

Health Perspectives in Salvadoran American Communities

HEALTH ISSUES

Many of the medical and health services targeted to immigrants and especially those offered to undocumented immigrants have been threatened by the anti-immigrant hysteria of the U.S. government since the early 1990s. One consequence is the restrictions that do not allow undocumented immigrants or their U.S.-born children to receive medical services or food stamps. The Central American population in the United States has special health and nutrition needs as many recent immigrants suffer from a variety of medical problems such as parasitic infections, gastroenteritis, malnutrition, and tuberculosis. They have high mortality rates and/or mental health problems. Until recently only a small number of social workers, psychologists, and psychiatrists had studied the mental health problems of Central American immigrants.

Many health issues and concerns are unique to Salvadoran populations residing in the United States. Salvadoran immigrants face at least four major health problems. The first and perhaps the most important problem area is the lack of significant scientific, sociological, and cultural research studies that provide data with respect to the health conditions experienced by the various Salvadoran communities in the United States. The lack of research studies also have created a void in understanding the idiosyncrasies present in the cultural patterns of Salvadoran populations in the different Salvadoran communities throughout the United States. There is also a lack of understanding on the part of health-related institutions and providers of the historical, social, economic, and political experiences that affected Salvadorans while living in Central America and eventually in the relocation in the United States. Finally, there is also a lack of access to health services for low-income and undocumented Salvadorans for the effective treatment of illness, diseases, and disabilities.

Regarding the lack of scientific research studies that address the health perspectives of Salvadoran populations in the United States, it is well known that incidence and disease rates differ within the various Hispanic populations; some populations may have a higher cancer or diabetes rate than others. It is also suspected that degree and incidence of disease increase as a result of generational issues and the length of residence in the United States. For example, the health patterns of a second-generation Salvadoran American individual may be somewhat similar to the higher rates of disease experienced by non-Hispanics. The lack of data on health issues related to Salvadoran populations in this country may be explained by lack of financial resources and funding for projects.[1] The lack of data on Salvadoran populations may also stem from the fact that a large percentage of this population does not have legal immigration status, and, therefore, they live marginalized from the mainstream society. Often they refuse to seek or accept government services or participate in official government data collection efforts out of fear that their participation in these programs might negatively impact the present or future immigration applications or legalization efforts.[2] Most of the available health-related research includes some Hispanic population identifiers, but most of the group ethnicity data are organized according to Mexicans, Puerto Ricans, Cubans, Central and South Americans, or other. The Salvadoran identifiers are lumped together with those of other Central and South American ethnic groups, even though there are great ethnic and cultural differences among these groups. The lack of data on the health issues, disability, and incidence of death among Salvadoran populations in the United States is a major problem for this community. Without relevant studies and data, health problems that require immediate attention cannot be identified and addressed, and therefore, objectives targeting the improvement of the health conditions and progress toward the reduction or elimination of these health problems cannot be measured.

The fact that most Salvadorans in the United States are of low-income status puts them at risk to be afflicted by illnesses that characteristically affect other low-income populations. Poverty affects a person's prospects for long and healthy life by increasing the chances of infant mortality, developmental problems in children, chronic disease, and traumatic death. The risk of death from heart disease is more than 25 percent higher for low-income people than for the general population, and the incidence of cancer increases as family income decreases, with survival rates lower for low-income cancer patients. Infectious diseases, such as HIV, AIDS, and tuberculosis, are commonly found among the poor.

The leading causes of death among Hispanics show a number of differences between their health perspectives and that of the general U.S. population. Heart disease and cancer are the leading diseases affecting Hispanic populations, but their death rates from heart disease and cancer are actually lower than for non-Hispanics. Diabetes also ranks high among the illnesses affecting Hispanic populations, and the research shows that genetic disposition, traditional diet, and lifestyle are important factors for the high rates in this population. Obesity is common among Salvadorans and especially among middle age and elderly men and women. Traditional dietary patterns are the most important cause for this obesity, as Salvadoran diet is high in carbohydrates and starches, very few vegetables are used, and many foods are often fried in lard.

When Salvadoran immigrants initially relocate in a new society, social, cultural, or economic pressures may have a negative impact on their health. For example, living in a new cultural environment where English is spoken instead of Spanish can create serious stresses for a Spanish-speaking immigrant. Salvadorans may experience difficulty learning English; they may find themselves unemployed for a significant amount of time; they may also experience changes in their standard of living; they may find themselves isolated, lonely, or homesick with very few friends around them; or just the experience of raising a family in a new social and cultural environment may create unwanted stresses on an individual or a family.

As a direct result of the migration processes and the dynamics of cultural adaptation and social adjustment in a new society, Salvadorans reportedly suffer from a number of physical ailments such as high blood pressure, sudden increase/decrease in blood pressure, headaches, increased pulse rate, backaches, stiff neck, muscle tension, nausea, vomiting, upset stomach and diarrhea, difficulty sleeping or eating, prolonged tiredness, as well as other ailments. They also experience psychological problems such as confusion, inability to think clearly, restlessness, depression, irritability and nervousness, anxiety, phobias, nightmares, and worries about day to day survival issues such as money, safety, and guilt for having left their home country. Some of the most severe problems faced by Salvadoran immigrants are alcohol dependency and drug abuse—both from pharmaceutical medications and street drugs.

There are a few reports that have documented the incidence of tuberculosis and other infectious tropical diseases among Salvadoran immigrants and refugees who had been already eradicated for years in the United States. These infectious diseases were reportedly spreading in many Salvadoran regions that

were severely impacted by frequent military actions and the forced relocation of large segments of the population in refugee camps run by the United
Nations and the Catholic Church. The unsanitary health and environmental
conditions in the combat zones, rural communities, and in the refugee camps
became a serious threat to large segments of the Salvadoran population during
the civil war. Many Salvadoran and other Central American immigrants and
refugees who arrived in the United States during the 1980s were afflicted by
or had been exposed to a wide range of infectious tropical illnesses. The great
majority of hospitals, clinics, and medical doctors in the United States were
not prepared to handle the influx of new immigrant and refugee populations
and the wide range of medical problems that they had brought with them.

There are also other significant problems affecting the health perspectives
of Salvadoran populations, such as their access to relevant information on
health and disease prevention. Salvadoran populations are often exposed to
national public health education campaigns conducted through the mainstream media or Spanish language media. However, these health campaigns
are not designed to address the particular linguistic, cultural, or communication needs of the Salvadoran community.

Another major problem is the access of Salvadoran populations to services
for the treatment of disease and disability. Their limited access to services
may be attributed to a variety of financial, linguistic, cultural, and legal barriers. Health insurance coverage is rare among needy working-class or undocumented Salvadorans, and a large percentage of the Salvadoran population do
not qualify for government health benefits such as Medicare or Medicaid,
despite their status as legal permanent residents. Linguistic barriers continue
to exist because of the inability of many health-care institutions to provide or
make available culturally competent bilingual health care employees or translators. And sometimes, even when health-care institutions provide informational publications or physician's instructions in Spanish, the high rate of
illiteracy among Salvadoran populations makes these publications useless.

Cultural barriers are also created from deeply ingrained health philoso-
phies, attitudes, and practices that have developed over the centuries. These
beliefs and practices, which include religiously based fatalism, herbal medicines, and self-prescribed and obtained pharmaceutical medications, tend to
impede or replace the appropriate medical care. Many of these beliefs and
practices are common in Salvadoran rural and urban working-class populations and are retained after their resettlement in the United States. It is
quite common for Salvadorans to consult relatives and friends about health,
illness, pain, and disability issues before seeking professional medical help.

It is common practice to get home remedies or pharmaceutical medications without a prescription from friends and relatives who had similar symptoms. This practice leads to serious health problems and risks, as an illness may be misdiagnosed, and an untrained individual may prescribe and administer the wrong medication, leading to further complications.

Because a large percentage of the Salvadoran immigrant population does not have legal status, they also encounter many legal barriers in the process of seeking medical services. These problems range from fears of deportation by immigration officials when an immigrant goes to a medical facility and uses the existing health services and benefits, to the denial of services because of their undocumented immigrant status. Because of fear of being apprehended and sent back to El Salvador, only a few undocumented Salvadorans use medical and social services available through community refugee centers. In most instances they do not seek help until the problem becomes a serious emergency. Some undocumented Salvadorans suffer from serious emotional disorders but seldom seek therapy. They do not voluntarily go for psychiatric evaluation and treatment. In most cases the family or friends bring them against their will to community clinics or hospitals.

Clínica Romero Staff members. Los Angeles, CA. Photo courtesy of Clínica Romero.

A few health programs and clinics have been started in various Salvadoran communities throughout the country. These collaborative efforts have been an effective way to address the financial, linguistic, cultural, and legal barriers to health care for the Salvadoran population. La Clínica del Pueblo in Washington, D.C., Clínica Romero in Los Angeles, and the CARECEN dental clinic in San Francisco serve as successful models for Salvadoran communities in providing health services to needy Salvadorans and other Latino immigrants.

MENTAL HEALTH ISSUES

Because of the pervasive violence that has affected many regions in El Salvador since the early 1980s, many Salvadoran immigrants to the United States have experienced direct and indirect psychological trauma. Most socio-political studies of the recent Salvadoran history agree that the civil war fought in El Salvador during the 1980s was the main social force to have driven the recent Salvadoran migrations into the United States. The high intensity warfare tended to concentrate in specific rural and urban regions of the country, which may have provoked a select migration of people at risk for post-traumatic stress disorders (PTSDs) or psychosocial trauma. The war left more than 75,000 people killed and more than 9,000 disappeared. Most of these were noncombatants killed by military missions carried out by the Salvadoran army and its paramilitary forces trained and financed by the United States. The arbitrary detention or abduction, followed by the disappearance, of the victim became a common practice of the security forces in Latin American countries governed under the Doctrine of National Security. In El Salvador, this tactic took on a distinct dimension: the objective was to eliminate the "subversive" and to instill terror in his/her family and neighbors with the use of irregular forces, such as death squads. The uncertainty about who would be the next victim served to give the general impression of absolute control and impunity. For those not familiar with the peculiarities of the Salvadoran conflict it may sound like an overstatement when claims are made that every Salvadoran family had a relative die as a direct result of the general conditions of war. All Salvadorans have been deeply impacted by the effects of the war, and that impact is rooted on the level of involvement in the conflict, area of residence, occupation, or family relations.

It is important to note the extent of the transnational cultural and social experiences faced by Salvadoran populations outside the Central American region. The events that are happening in the home country always have a deep and serious impact to those populations living abroad. The events can be of a social, cultural, political, or economic nature, and they may have either positive or negative influences on the psychological welfare of the immigrants. In addition, natural catastrophes or man-made disasters can have a devastating effect on the populations at home and also to those living abroad. For example, at the time of the 1986 earthquake in San Salvador many working class communities were leveled by the seismic activity leaving thousands of people wounded or dead. At the same time, the impact of the earthquake was severely felt by Salvadoran communities all over the world. Salvadorans struggled with the fact that little information was coming out of El Salvador with news about relatives or friends, and a high incidence of emotional trauma and psychological crises were reported in Salvadoran communities all over the united States.

Many Salvadoran immigrants were severely impacted by the war at home. Even though they left El Salvador in the early 1980s, they also manifested many of the symptoms of war trauma and psychosocial trauma manifested by their countrymen in Central America. Individuals who themselves or their relatives have been victims of political violence in El Salvador frequently manifest various forms of psychological problems upon their arrival and settlement in the United States. Torture victims often suffer PTSD exhibited as severe depression, guilt, nightmares, hyper-alertness, insomnia, suicidal tendencies, and withdrawal. Psychiatric evaluations of Central Americans conducted by refugee centers in the San Francisco Bay Area, Los Angeles, Boston, and New York have concluded that a large number of their clients suffer from PTSD.

These individuals often migrate alone, are separated from family and friends, and have few relatives or friends in the host society. All that is part of their social and cultural world is part of the past. Salvadoran immigrants state that the separation from their family, country, and familiar surroundings was the most emotionally distressing to them. Involuntary and sudden departures do not allow for mourning of dead relatives and friends, or for gradual changes in their established lifestyles. All familiarity and sense of belonging are lost in the process, bringing emotional and identity problems for the immigrant. The immigrants often relive past experiences in El Salvador to the point of becoming obsessive and disturbed. Sometimes solitude and the recurring memories bring on suicidal thoughts. The psychological disorders negatively impact marital and family relationships. Conflicts, depression, alcohol and drug abuse, frustration, family violence, separation, and divorce are some of the most recurring consequences of the emotional disorders reported for these individuals.

Healing the scars of war and violence of these Salvadoran immigrants and refugees is a difficult task. For many of the relatives of the 75,000 civilians who were killed since the 1980s, healing takes on a different and profound meaning. One way to approach it is that families will have to perceive that their loss and pain were not in vain. Because *el dolor* (their pain) was collective, healing would have to be in a dialectic process that comes from the social to the particular individual situation.

It is important to reframe the commonly held ideas about mental health therapy among Salvadoran populations. Many Salvadorans are not completely familiar with individual-based approaches to mental health and psychological treatment rather than family or community approaches. They might believe that healthy and sane persons do not seek the services of psychologists; only those who are mentally ill do so. Because of the stigma attached to mental-health issues and services, Salvadorans tend to perceive them as services exclusively for those who have the most serious mental disorders and require supervised living or institutionalization. Less extreme disorders, for which effective treatments are available, tend to be viewed as not requiring professional intervention. Because of this and other cultural factors, Salvadorans tend to express psychological distress through somatic symptoms and seek medical services for stress-related conditions.

NOTES

1. Public Health Service, U.S. Department of Health and Human Services, *Healthy People 2000: National Health Promotion and Disease Prevention Objectives*—full report with commentary (DHHS Publication No. (PHS) 91–50213) (Washington, D.C.: U.S. Government Printing Office, 1990).

2. Central American Strategic Planning Committee, *Health Committee Strategic Plan,* project funded by the VESPER Society, Oakland, California, May 1995.

7

Intergroup Issues Affecting Salvadoran American Communities

ETHNIC RELATIONS IN LOS ANGELES

Most Salvadorans who have relocated in Los Angeles have resettled in the Pico Union, Westlake, and McArthur Park areas. The Pico Union is a tough place to live as high levels of gang activity and drug dealing have affected the life in the neighborhood since the early 1990s. Unemployment is high in this community and Salvadorans as well as other residents lack representation in the political life of L.A. Many Salvadoran and Guatemalan immigrants live in these ethnically mixed neighborhoods in overcrowded apartments, which are owned by absentee landlords. The immigrants fear the gangs and criminal activity in the streets and are extremely distrustful of the local authorities and law enforcement agencies. Most arrived in the United States within the last decade, mainly as refugees from the civil wars in Central America and the Mexican economic crisis of the early 1980s.

South-central Los Angeles has long been a predominantly African American neighborhood, but since the early 1980s, this community has experienced a dramatic influx of Latin Americans, many of them undocumented Mexicans and Central Americans. During this time, Central Americans began moving into the Pico-Union neighborhood, just west of downtown Los Angeles and north of the south-central area, but as that area became overcrowded, Latino families relocated south of the Santa Monica freeway to south-central L.A. African Americans moved out of the south-central neighborhoods to better communities to the west or south, and at the same time, Central American and Mexican immigrants moved in as they were attracted by the affordability of real estate in the area.[1]

Between the late-1970s and the early 1990s, the number of Latinos, increased by 119 percent in south-central L.A., while the number of African Americans declined by 17 percent. The 1990 census showed that south-central Los Angeles was 45 percent Hispanic and 48 percent African American. More than half of the infants born at the Martin Luther King Jr. Hospital are born to Latina mothers.

But there were no Latino elected officials from south-central Los Angeles, partly because many of the residents are recently arrived immigrants and are not U.S. citizens and, therefore, they have no voting rights. A handful of agencies that provided social services to Latino immigrants were found in the area at that time. Even in churches where the congregations are becoming more Hispanic, parishioners barely speak to newcomers because of the language barrier.

On April 29, 1992, riots began in Los Angeles after the verdict of the Rodney King trial, in which four white police officers were acquitted of beating him. It appears that many Central American residents of the south-central area and other parts of Los Angeles were affected by the violence to a certain extent because they were not well established in the communities. Many Central American immigrants also suffered from the same depressed economic conditions as others who were rioting and looting. It was not just an African American problem; the reality was that people of color in general were dissatisfied with the unequal treatment of ethnic minority groups by the city government and law enforcement agencies.

The Los Angeles Police Department (LAPD) reported that about a third of those arrested were Latinos and that many were undocumented aliens who were immediately turned over to the INS for deportation. The Central American immigrant community was seriously concerned over actions carried out by the LAPD. According to INS reports, undocumented immigrants accounted for more than 1,200 of the nearly 15,000 people arrested in the riots. There were 477 undocumented aliens picked up and handed to the INS by the LAPD, 360 were from Mexico; 62 from El Salvador; 35 from Guatemala; and 14 from Honduras. There were 58 people who died in the riots; 19 of them, more than a third, were Latinos and hundreds more were injured and left homeless. Of the businesses destroyed, 30–40 percent were owned by Latinos. But African Americans and Latinos were not the only participants in the looting and violence, as Whites and Asians were also arrested. As a response to the arrests and deportations, the governments of Mexico, El Salvador, Guatemala, and Honduras joined together to ask Mayor Tom Bradley to respect immigrants' human rights, regardless of their legal status.

Elected Latino officials were eager to distance themselves from the Latino immigrant enclaves of Pico-Union and southern Los Angeles that were involved in the violence. Most elected Latino officials, who for the most part are of Mexican descent, have few connections with recently created Central American Spanish-speaking immigrant communities. Central American community leaders stated that the Central American immigrants were ignored during the painful post-riot recovery and urged Latino elected officials to represent all Latinos, not only those that were citizens. And in reality, elected Latino officials placed most of the blame on the Central American immigrants for the violence that affected L.A. for three days.[2]

After the riots a great deal of tension existed between the Latino, African American, and Asian communities. And for the first time, a dialogue opened up between different ethnic community leaders to try to develop viable solutions to the problems that created the social violence.

THE STREET GANG PHENOMENON IN SALVADORAN COMMUNITIES

Most Salvadoran immigrants and refugees who arrived in the United States during the Salvadoran civil war in the 1980s and early '90s resettled in already established Latino communities in Los Angeles. These neighborhoods were located in the territory under the jurisdiction of the ramparts division of the LAPD.

The new Salvadoran immigrants were perceived as outsiders and were not readily accepted into these traditionally Mexican neighborhoods. They were often the targets of vicious attacks from the active Mexican gangs. Soon thereafter, young Salvadorans began to organize smaller scale gangs in their neighborhoods—a significant number had received military training in El Salvador either in the Salvadoran army or the FMLN. They were able to train the new Salvadoran gang members with a high level of military discipline and efficiency. They eventually formed what became known as "La Mara Salvatrucha," or MS13, the best-organized Salvadoran gang in Los Angeles. The word *mara* is used in El Salvador to refer to a group of friends that hang around together. It originates from the word *marabunta,* which is the name given to the Amazonian soldier ants that destroy everything in their path in the rainforest. *Salvatrucha* is a slang word for Salvadoran.

During the early days of this youth gang, their activities were designed to protect themselves from the actions of the Mexican gangs, but eventually they began to demand payments from local merchants and neighbors in return for protection. The highly organized gang expanded rapidly through other parts of California and the United States, and soon it became well known for its ruthlessness and extreme violence. La Mara Salvatrucha has now expanded its activities and territories from California and Washington, D.C. to New York, Florida, Maryland, New Jersey, Nevada, Colorado, Texas, the Carolinas, Utah, Oregon, Illinois, Michigan, Georgia, Oklahoma, Alaska, Canada, Mexico, and other Central American countries. According to FBI reports, the Mara Salvatrucha is active in 31 states and has thousands of members in Central America.[3] Most recently the gang members have expanded their activities to rural communities where they may control larger territories that have weaker law enforcement agencies. They have relocated in new communities where Central Americans and other Latinos are rapidly moving to work in a variety of blue-collar jobs in giant food factories and food processing plants.

The transnational impact of the gang is highly significant. Gang members in the United States maintain close ties with their counterparts in El Salvador. There have been many reports in the Salvadoran media how Mara Salvatrucha gang members in Los Angeles have been responsible for numerous crimes committed in El Salvador and other Central American countries. The contact and levels of communication between gang members in the United States and El Salvador are important because of the trade that is carried out involving military weapons, munitions, handguns, drugs, and smuggled stolen cars and other illicit activities. It has been reported that a high percentage of the cars driven in El Salvador were actually stolen in the United States by Salvadoran gang members.

When La Mara Salvatrucha was originally created, only Salvadorans could join, but as time has passed, other Central and South Americans have been allowed to join its ranks. They have also allowed African Americans to join them. But still the great majority of its membership is of Salvadoran origin. Most members are young people, ranging from 11 to 40 years of age.

The gang members identify themselves with numerous tattoos all over their bodies and often use the letters "MS" or the number 13 (*trece* in Spanish) and are often referred to as the MS13. They are also identified with the "Sureño" gangs, making reference to their Southern California origins and as opposed to the other gangs that originated in northern California. They have been rivals with other Southern California gangs such as the 18th Street gang in Los Angeles, but in recent years Salvadorans have also joined the 18th Street gang and have also re-created the gang structure and rivalries in El Salvador.

Law enforcement agencies and the judicial systems have arrested, incarcerated, or deported Salvadoran gang members. Many Mara Salvatrucha gang members remain illegally in the United States or are facing deportation to El Salvador. When gang members are deported to El Salvador, they face a very difficult experience, because many of them came to the United States when they were young children, and they know very little about life in Central America. In addition, the gang members are not welcome by the mainstream Salvadoran society. They are seen as undesirables and antisocial individuals.

Since the early 1990s, young Salvadoran immigrants who were involved in the L.A. gang scene and were convicted of felony crimes were deported by the INS and were sent back to El Salvador. The Mara Salvatrucha was originally created in Los Angeles, but their deported gang members recreated their Los Angeles turfs and rivalries in El Salvador and recruited many young Salvadorans to join their ranks. Salvadoran sociologists have stated that for every gang member who was deported from the United States, a new group of 20–25 young men could be recruited, trained, and incorporated into the gang lifestyle by each gang member who had been deported. The deported gang members began to recruit new members in the working class middle and high schools and in the poor neighborhoods in San Salvador. Soon thereafter, the gangs also began to spread their influence to rural communities and provincial cities, as well as to other Central American countries.

Salvadoran police have estimated that El Salvador has about 17,000 gang members. Other reliable sources say it may be double that number. In a period of just more than 10 years, Salvadoran society has been seriously impacted by the new youth gang violence brought about by those gang members who were deported from the United States. Gang violence in Central America, the United States, and Mexico has become a major challenge for law enforcement agencies. The violent acts they commit are quite serious, even when carried out by 10-year-olds. Some gangs have been involved in extortion and mass murders. Some have been linked to organized crime in the United States and El Salvador. Salvadoran government officials have stated that gangs are responsible for 80 percent of the violent deaths in that country. Gangs have become the most destabilizing factor in Salvadoran society and in Salvadoran communities in the United States since the civil war ended in 1992.

During October 2003, the Salvadoran government passed what has become known as the "anti-Mara" law. Thousands of young men fitting the physical descriptions of gang members have been arrested in El Salvador as part of the "Mano Dura" (hard hand) policies of the ruling ARENA Party, which has targeted gang members and promised to put an end to all gangs. Article 29 of the new anti-Mara legislation states that individuals deported for gang activity can be arrested as they return to El Salvador, regardless of whether they have committed any crimes in their country of origin. Large numbers of recent deportees have been arrested in El Salvador under the new law because they are suspected gang members.

Mara Salvatrucha graffiti in San Francisco, CA. Photo by Carlos Texca.

These policies are being conducted to complement the recent crackdown on gangs and, specifically, La Mara Salvatrucha in Los Angeles by the new police chief, William J. Bratton, who as the head of the New York Police Department carried out the "Zero Tolerance" programs against gangs in New York City. In addition, in March 2003, General James T. Hill, the head of U.S. Southern Command, while discussing terrorism in Latin America, included gangs as one of the most important sources of terrorism in the region. This broadening of the definition of a terrorist has created a controversy in regard to the social and political role of governments in the United States and Central America in trying to control the gang problem in the region. Gang members, or *mareros,* are certainly not terrorists in the strictest sense of the word. Their violent acts are not politically motivated. In most cases, they target their own or rival gang members, not noncombatants or innocent civilians as terrorists do.

On the positive side, a few years ago former gang members and community activists in Los Angeles and San Salvador created an organization called "Homies Unidos," with an emphasis on gang intervention and prevention. They are involved in the Latino community by holding gang prevention discussions with youths at the local schools, churches, and community centers. They work with the gangs in facilitating conflict resolutions and truces between rival gangs. They also have created a tattoo removal program and help involve the youth in art and cultural programs as the means of rehabilitating gang members and preventing further gang activities in the Central American communities. They have been very effective in helping former gang members in their rehabilitation and reincorporation into society by providing counseling, guidance, and employment referral services to youth at risk. It is important to note that many see prevention and educational programs as necessary tools to help slow down gang activities in the Central American communities in the United States. Law enforcement and incarceration are not necessarily the only solutions to this serious social problem presently faced by Salvadoran and Central American communities in the United States and in Central America.

NOTES

1. Hector Tobar, "No Strength in Numbers for L.A.'s Divided Latinos," Metro Desk, *Los Angeles Times,* part A, page 1, column 1, September 1, 1992.

2. George Ramos and Tracy Wilkerson, "Unrest Widens Rift in Diverse Latino Population," Metro Desk, *Los Angeles Times,* part A, page 1, column 5, May 8, 1992.

3. Mathew Brzezinski, "Hillbangers," *The New York Times Magazine* (August 15, 2004): 38–43.

8

Impact on U.S. Society and Culture

PARTICIPATION IN THE LABOR FORCE

Employment opportunities are a major factor affecting the social adaptation and economic stability of immigrant communities. Immigrants with legal status, high levels of education, and good English-language skills have been able to integrate into many sectors of the labor market. Those with legalized immigration status and low levels of education have some opportunity to pursue education and training, but educational programs for adults are limited. Because employment opportunities so closely depend on an individual's immigration status, the economic opportunities available to undocumented workers are limited. Even for the educated, especially those with limited language proficiency, jobs are most often found in factories, construction and janitorial firms, the hotel and restaurant industry or in domestic services—sectors where undocumented workers are vulnerable to exploitation and paid low wages.

Many immigrants find employment within an ethnic enclave, in the secondary labor market, or in domestic labor. Employment is secured through contacts established in their ethnic network, from family and friends who find jobs for new arrivals at their place of employment, or in places known to hire undocumented workers. For Central Americans, church based groups and nonprofit community agencies have provided job counseling, referral services, and job networks. In the current anti-immigrant climate, undocumented immigration status is the most serious problem faced by most Central American immigrants. Legislation, such as Proposition 187 in

California, seriously impacts the economic, social, and cultural experience of the undocumented Latino population.

Immigrants bring economic benefits to the new homeland. As in the case of California, large-scale immigration has not depressed the local economy and perhaps has increased the per capita income in the state. The economic benefits outweigh the costs, which primarily come from the immigrants' use of public services such as schools and hospitals. Conservative and anti-immigrant groups have continued to hold the view that undocumented workers do in fact have a negative effect on the economic system because they create unfair competition for jobs. They argue that the undocumented person takes jobs at the bottom of the economic structure, but strives harder, and in many instances does not hold one but various jobs to make ends meet, therefore depleting the available pool of jobs for the native worker.

Central Americans, both men and women, have high rates of labor force participation. However, the population is poorly integrated into the U.S. labor market with the vast majority of its members disproportionately employed in low-wage sectors. Their unemployment rate is 5.1 percent, which is lower than the rate experienced by other Central Americans, with the exception of Nicaraguans, who show a 4 percent unemployment rate. The low unemployment rate for Nicaraguans may be attributed to the fact that they have a much higher educational level at 12 years of completed schooling as well as the fact that they have been in this country longer. Guatemalans have completed on average 9.8 years of schooling and show a 7.9 percent unemployment rate, while Hondurans have accomplished 10.4 years of schooling and show a 10.8 percent unemployment rate. The Honduran unemployment rates may be attributed to their relatively short length of residence in the United States and their lower levels of English-language proficiency. Most Central Americans (approximately 85 percent) have jobs requiring less education. In 1990, only 9 percent of Central Americans were employed in the managerial and professional sector. Most Salvadorans are employed in the service industry; men are often working as bus boys, dishwashers, cooks, janitors, and unskilled jobs in the hotel and restaurant industry. Others work in construction, gardening, landscaping, auto mechanics, as well as day laborers. Women are employed in domestic services, working as baby-sitters, house cleaners, cooks, and live-in maids. Women also work in the hotel and restaurant industries as cleaning and laundry maids and cooks. Others perform manual labor in factories. Many other Salvadorans work in the informal sectors selling goods in the streets that range from traditional foods prepared at home to video tapes, audio cassettes and CD's, flowers, and souvenir clothing.

As a direct consequence of low earnings many Central American families are quite poor. Most would be described as "working poor" because these are families where adults are working full-time but their wages are not high enough to lift them out of poverty. In 1990, 25 percent of Central American families with children were living below the poverty level. Among Central Americans, rates of poverty are highest among Honduran, Salvadoran, and Guatemalan families. Importantly, rates of poverty are highest among families whose members are not citizens. The population also includes a small percentage of families and households whose incomes are higher. In 1990, 15 percent of Central American households had incomes of more than $50,000 and 4.6 percent had incomes of more than $75,000. In 2000, the major Central American groups had average earnings of less than $10,000 per year, which is roughly equivalent to that of Puerto Ricans, though they are less likely to fall below the poverty line. Salvadorans were reported to have average earnings of $9,631, with approximately 20.8 percent falling below the poverty line.

It is possible to observe more similarities across socioeconomic class status rather than in national identity issues between different Central American populations. Large numbers of individuals of various Central American origins presently living in the United States come from middle or working class backgrounds. They include teachers, high school and university students, secretaries, accountants, homemakers, domestic workers, office workers, and skilled factory workers. They also include large numbers of much poorer, rural agricultural workers who arrived in the United States in the 1980s escaping political persecution, forced relocation, or the unsafe political climate in their native rural communities. Throughout and across various Central American countries, working class and poor populations have strong similarities in their social and cultural experiences and have very little in common with upper-class social and cultural experiences. It is important to take into account the various settlement patterns of Salvadorans in the United States as well as the social migration networks and hometown associations as they reflect more similarities based on their origins in El Salvador.

SALVADORAN FOOD IN THE UNITED STATES

As a direct result of the Salvadoran migrations to this country, Salvadoran restaurants have opened in many Latino and Central American communities all over the United States. Most Salvadoran restaurants also serve Mexican or other Latin American foods to complement their menus. This is not done because there is a lack of demand for Salvadoran dishes but to accommodate the demand for Mexican, Peruvian, Guatemalan, or Nicaraguan dishes based on the population make-up of the local communities. Salvadoran restaurants in the United States do not serve many of the food delicacies found in El Salvador such as iguana or turtle eggs, roasted iguana meat, and armadillo meat. Most restaurants do not serve home-style cooking either but have adopted a standard menu that includes the most common Salvadoran dishes.

Corn tortillas are the main Salvadoran staple food, served with every meal. Salvadoran tortillas are smaller and much thicker than Mexican hand-made tortillas; they actually look like thick pancakes. They are not to be rolled like the thin machine-made Mexican tortillas; instead, people put their food on top and eat them as one would a tostada, or pieces of the tortilla are cut with the fingers and the food is scooped up with a fork and a piece of tortilla. It is not proper etiquette to cut a tortilla with a knife; it must be cut with the fingers. It is a common Salvadoran belief that it is sinful to cut a tortilla with a knife; this belief may be traced to the ancient pre-Hispanic belief that corn was also a divine grain. Compared with Guatemalan tortillas, Salvadoran tortillas are much larger. A typical Salvadoran breakfast may include corn tortillas, eggs, fried sweet ripe plantains, refried beans, and *queso duro,* a type of dry, hard, Salvadoran cheese.

The national dish of El Salvador are *pupusas,* a flat, round corn dough tortilla filled either with cheese, *chicharrón* (deep-fried pork), or *revueltas* (refried beans). Cheese *pupusas* may include *loroco,* a tasty aromatic flower that adds a peculiar flavor to the *pupusas.* A recent adaptation to the U.S. diet has included *pupusas* with zucchini and green peppers. Traditionally, only women make *pupusas,* and it is a true art to be able to make good ones. A handful of corn dough is shaped into a ball in the hands, then a depression is made in the dough with the knuckles, the filling is placed in the hole and the ball of dough is carefully closed, the ball is next patted with the palms until the desired shape is formed without letting the filling spill out. The *pupusa* is finally cooked on a *comal* (griddle) until fully cooked. *Pupusas* are served with *curtido,* a mixture of boiled cabbage, with onions, carrots, peppers, oregano, salt, and pepper that is pickled in white vinegar.

Other typical dishes found in most Salvadoran restaurants in the United States include *yuca con chicharrón,* boiled yucca or sweet manioc served with deep fried pork and Salvadoran tomato and chile salsa; *panes con chumpe,* a Salvadoran turkey sandwich served with romaine lettuce, cucumbers, radishes, watercress, and a special turkey gravy called *recaudo*; and *bistec encebollado,* steak with caramelized onions served with rice and beans. Another Salvadoran delicacy is fried ripe plantains. They are served with refried beans and sour cream. Plantains are also prepared as dessert empanadas or *rellenitos* as they

Woman making *pupusas*. Photo by Carlos Texca.

are called in Guatemala, in which mashed ripe plantains are shaped into little turnovers stuffed with milk pudding or refried beans and deep-fried until they are fully cooked. There is also *casamiento* or marriage, a vegetarian dish made with a mixture of fried whole beans and rice, which may be served with eggs, avocado, thick cream, and a piece of *queso duro* on the side.

Salvadoran tamales are a bit different from their Mexican counterparts. There are different types of tamales such as *tamales de sal* (salty tamales) that are made from a corn dough mixture that is filled with beef, chicken, olives, onions, potatoes, bell peppers, and are wrapped in banana leaves. Salvadorans also make *tamales de azúcar* (sweet tamales) that are filled with chicken, raisins, a prune, and cinnamon. And there are also *tamales de elote*

Pupuseria in the Mission District, San Francisco, CA. Photo by Carlos Texca.

(sweet corn tamales) made from tender fresh corn. Tamales are the traditional foods served for many family fiestas such as baptisms, first communions, birthdays, and funerals.

Salvadoran traditional menus include a wide variety of *frescos,* natural sweet drinks made from a number of tropical fruits such as tamarindo, mango, cantaloupe, marañón, or cashew fruit; or drinks made from ground seeds and spices such as *horchata,* a drink made from toasted ground pumpkin and gourd seeds, and *cebada,* a barley drink with cinnamon. Most meals are accompanied by a light and sweet coffee brew or sweet hot chocolate. There is also corn *atol de elote,* a sweet drink made from fresh corn that is considered a divine ritual drink by the ancient and contemporary indigenous cultures of Mexico and Central America. Common alcoholic drinks include light beers, Pilsener, Suprema, and Regia that are distributed throughout the United States. Kola Shampan, a popular Salvadoran soft drink, is also found in the restaurant menus in the United States.

SALVADORAN AMERICAN ARTS AND CULTURE

Central American regional associations are sometimes dedicated to the religious worship of a Patron Saint or a special Catholic deity. The regional associations take charge of the planning, organizing, fundraising, and festivities to honor their sacred symbols. Some of these events take place in cooperation with Catholic Church priests and officials while others are organized in social clubs, parks, or cultural centers. Such are the examples in the Nicaraguan community with organizations and individuals dedicated to the worship of Our Lady of the Conception (La Purísima Concepción), or the Fiesta of Saint Dominic (Santo Domingo). Salvadorans have regional associations dedicated to "El Dívino Salvador del Mundo," the Savior of the World, the patron saint of El Salvador, and they are responsible for the celebrations of "la bajada del Señor" during the August festivities. In Los Angeles, for example, the Salvadoran American National Association commissioned a replica of the original icon of the Salvador del Mundo that is housed at the National Cathedral in San Salvador so as to make the celebration more authentic. Just like in the celebrations in San Salvador, the image is dressed in a purple robe as it stands on top of a globe of the world. The statue is lowered into the globe and a few minutes later it reemerges dressed in white to represent the transfiguration of Christ. This celebration brings together the Salvadoran community and has become a symbol of the continuation of the Salvadoran experience outside the Central American borders.[1]

Other Salvadoran festivities that are organized and celebrated by the regional associations include the Independence celebrations on September 15th and the San Miguel Carnival in November. The Salvadoran community also celebrates the Day of the Cross on May 3rd, and it is an important festivity in El Salvador as it marks the beginning of the rainy season and the greening of the landscape. Some communities have adopted the festivity to celebrate the Salvadoran immigrant experience in the United States, and it matches the Mexican celebrations of Cinco de Mayo.

In recent years Salvadoran business owners have formed various chapters of the Salvadoran American Chamber of Commerce in a number of cities. They provide Salvadoran business enterprises with support, training, and assessment of their business plans. The Salvadoran American Chambers of Commerce are also engaged in organizing social events, cultural programs, and business seminars for Salvadoran professionals and businesses in their local communities. In addition, the Chambers of Commerce have sponsored numerous Salvadoran art exhibits throughout the most important Salvadoran communities in the United States.

Salvadoran American communities in the United States have a rich artistic and cultural expression. In every Salvadoran American community, there are individuals involved in every aspect of the arts—in painting, muralism, music, poetry, theater, and more.

For decades, the San Francisco Bay area has been a center for Salvadoran and Central American cultural and artistic development. Many Salvadoran artists, cultural workers, and intellectuals have worked together to create a strong cultural, social, artistic, and political agenda to further develop and promote Central American issues in the United States. A group of Salvadoran artists and students at San Francisco State University working together with other Mexican, Chicano, and Central American cultural workers were responsible for founding the Mission Cultural Center for Latino Arts (MCCLA) in the Mission district, the Latino enclave in San Francisco. This was an important development in the artistic experience of Central Americans and Latinos as the MCCLA provided space for a diversity of artistic disciplines from performance, music, dance, theater, graphic and plastic arts, and more.

Romeo Gilberto Osorio was the gallery director and helped create the largest Latino gallery space in the Bay Area available for the dissemination of Latino expression. Osorio was a graphic artist who also explored the arts thru drawing, painting, mural design, as well as creating works in plastic sculpture and design. In the 1990s, Osorio was the artistic editor for Revista VOCES, where his essays on Latino and Central American art criticism received a great deal of acclaim. During the past years, he has been the curator and director of

Romeo G. Osorio. Photo by Carlos Texca.

the Art Gallery at Piñata Art as well as the artistic director for *Revista Latino Vision*, an electronic internet arts magazine focusing on Latino Art in the United States and abroad.

Also living and working in San Francisco are the Cartagena brothers, Victor, Carlos, and Ricardo (Cachi). They are a trio of highly talented and internationally recognized brothers who use paintings and mixed media to represent the Salvadoran cultural and social experiences in El Salvador and in their local community.

Ricardo Cartagena, popularly known as "Cachi," was born in San Salvador in 1963. Just like his brothers, he was highly influenced by his mother, María Ardón, who trained as an artist in El Salvador. During his adolescent years,

Cachi Cartagena. Photo by Carlos Texca.

Cachi became involved in the artistic and political movements in El Salvador; and as a result he developed a strong commitment for the social causes of the poor in his country. By the end of 1981, he joined the revolutionary movement, and because of his activism, he was arrested. He was never tried by the Salvadoran court system and was forced to spend 10 years in prison as a political prisoner. During his imprisonment, he worked in the creative areas that he loved the most—painting, poetry, music, and wood sculpture. He was freed from prison after the signing of the Peace Accords in 1992 and in 1994 relocated to San Francisco as a political asylee. Cachi has said that he paints because painting sets him free, because he is obsessed with the feeling of freedom. Therefore, every time he produces art work, he experiences that feeling of being free. His work reflects his past and present experiences either of a political, emotional, or romantic nature, and the traumas experienced during his childhood, as well as his religious faith.

Carlos and Victor Cartagena are members of the artist collective known as Tamoanchan, the ancient pre-Hispanic place of origins. Their work includes paintings, mixed media, and installations that directly confront their memories

"Angel with the Moon" by Cachi Cartagena. Photo by Carlos Texca.

of the political struggles and experiences in Central America and the plight of the Central American immigrants in the United States. Their strong imagery sends a powerful message of the pain and anguish that is part of the spiritual, cultural, and social baggage carried by Central American immigrants. Just like Cachi, Carlos and Victor represent in their works the social issues experienced in the Latino and immigrant communities—homelessness, material waste and the excesses of a consumer society, the oppression experienced by immigrants, and the life in the barrio as well as the immigrant's longing for the home country. Victor has also been involved in producing set designs for local theater companies. This has exposed him to a new audience, and he has received positive reviews from art critics in this new endeavor.

Martivon Galindo. Photo courtesy of Ms. Galindo.

Martivón Galindo is a Salvadoran poet, university professor, political activist, and artist who also represents the suffering experienced by Salvadorans during the civil war and the struggles of Salvadoran immigrants living in the United States. Galindo graduated as an architect from National University in El Salvador and has a Ph.D. in Literature and Spanish Languages from the University of California at Berkeley. She is currently Associate Professor of Spanish and Latin American History at Holy Names College in Oakland, California.

"Untitled" by Martivon Galindo. Photo courtesy of Ms. Galindo.

She was a founder and directed for many years CODICES of San Francisco—a cultural center that researched and documented Salvadoran culture and art. Her poems, narratives, short stories, and critical essays have appeared in many publications in Mexico, El Salvador, and the United States. Since the 1990s, she has been producing engravings and mixed media.

Another important Salvadoran artist in the United States is Mario Bencastro. He was born in Ahuachapan, El Salvador in 1949 and lives in Washington, D.C. In 1977, he helped co-found "Magnet," a painters collective in New York. He has shown his works in the United States, Latin America, and Europe. After the 1979 military coup in El Salvador, Mario stopped painting and dedicated himself to poetry and narrative. In 1989, he finished his first novel, *A Shot in the Cathedral,* a book that describes the difficult times experienced by Salvadoran people in the years preceding the civil war and ends with the impact of the assassination of Archbishop Oscar Romero.

Bencastro has since received international recognition as an accomplished writer. His narratives are a vivid documentation of life in El Salvador during the brutal civil war and the Salvadoran immigrant experience and exile in the East Coast of the United States. His books *The Tree of Life: Stories of Civil War* and *Odyssey to the North* are powerful illustrations of the Salvadoran social, political, and cultural realities during the past 25 years.

Writer Jorge Argueta left El Salvador and relocated in San Francisco in 1980. His early years in this country were dramatically affected by the stresses of the migration and adaptation realities commonly faced by Salvadoran refugees. He worked at a local cafe frequented by poets, writers, and artists, and Argueta began to write poetry about his personal experience, love, and his surrounding environment. However, the stresses of his new life in San Francisco led him to drinking and the verge of collapse. But with the spiritual support of the native American church and the memory of the love that his Nahuat grandmother had given him, he was able to cope with the adaptation experience and began to write children's books that reflect the Salvadoran immigrant reality and the folk characters in the traditional children stories that are such an integral part of the Salvadoran culture. His book *Zipitío* is about the traditional goblin popular in Salvadoran folklore who comes at night to seduce young girls. This is a popular story that goes back to Salvadoran pre-Hispanic times.

His book *A Movie in My Pillow* represents San Francisco through the view of a newcomer Salvadoran boy. The book won him a 2001 Americas award for Children's and Young Adult Literature. Argueta's book *Xochitl and the Flowers* is also one of the first children's books about Salvadoran children's experiences in the United States. It tells the story of a Salvadoran family making a living selling flowers in the Mission District in San Francisco.

Leticia Hernández is part of the young Salvadoran writers movement in the United States. She was born in Hollywood, California, and is active in the Salvadoran communities of San Francisco and Los Angeles working with youth in the arts. Her poetry includes musical and performance elements that give her work a vibrant and innovative flavor while expressing her experiences as a Salvadoran American woman in the United States. Her poetry has been published in a number of literary journals, and her chapbook "Razor Edges of my Tongue" was published by Calaca Press and has received critical acclaim. Hernández's artistic work also includes drama and performance.

Hernández's work was also published in "Izote Vós," the first-ever collection of young Salvadoran American writing and visual art. Fourteen writers from San Francisco and Los Angeles ranging from ages 15 to 29 published their essay narratives, poems, and photographs depicting life in their communities and shared their family histories, war stories, and personal life experiences. Almost all of the writers were born in El Salvador; some came to the United States as infants or young children and some even as teenagers

Culture Clash is a highly acclaimed and talented comedy trio that was originally formed in 1984 during the Cinco de Mayo festivities in the Mission District in San Francisco and eventually relocated in Los Angeles. Herbert Siguenza and Ric Salinas, two of Culture Clash's members, were born in El Salvador and migrated to the United States as young children with their parents. The third member, Richard Montoya, is a Chicano born in California. Their work includes theatrical performances that encompass satire and a humorous discussion of Latino and mainstream politics, social issues, and cultural expressions. They have performed many comedy plays in Los Angeles, San Francisco, New York, Miami, and other cities. They have performed at South Coast Repertory, the Mark Taper Forum, Los Angeles Theatre Center, La Jolla Playhouse, the Japan American Theatre, Berkeley

Culture Clash. Photo courtesy of Culture Clash.

Repertory Theater, the Brava Theater, as well as off-Broadway Lincoln Center and the Kennedy Center. They have played at many major universities and colleges throughout the country.

In 1992, their play "A Bowl of Beings" premiered on PBS's Great Performances series and received critical acclaim. They opened up a door for Latinos on television with 30 episodes of Culture Clash that were broadcast during prime time by the Fox Broadcasting Network. This was the first ever half-hour sketch comedy for TV with a Latino theme that was executive produced and written by its stars. It aired in seven markets in the United States. Culture Clash members have appeared in the films *Encino Man* and *Hero*. The group co-produced, co-wrote, and starred in an award-winning 1992 short film entitled *Columbus on Trial* directed by Lourdes del Portillo.

Their first book, *Life, Death, and Revolutionary Comedy*, has been published by Theatre Communications Group and includes their plays "The Mission," "A Bowl of Beings," and "Radio Mambo."[2] They recently published another book, *Culture Clash in America*, and it includes their plays "Bordertown," "Nuyorican Stories," "Mission Magic Mystery Tour," and "Anthems."

NOTES

1. Valerie Orleans, "Professor studies 'La Bajada' among L.A. Salvadorans. California State University at Fullerton," *Dateline*, February 5, 2004.

2. Culture Clash in America, http://www.cultureclash.com.

Appendix 1: Notable Salvadorans in the United States

ANA SOL GUTIERREZ (1942–)

Educator and businesswoman Ana Sol Gutiérrez was born in El Salvador in 1942. She has lived for more than 40 years in the United States, has traveled extensively, and has worked in Switzerland, Venezuela, Bolivia, and Peru. She is trilingual, speaking fluent Spanish, English, and French.

Her commitment to education and public service continues with her active involvement in numerous national and local organizations. She was elected as a member of the Montgomery County Board of Education in Maryland in 1990. She has served both as president and vice-president of the Board and completed eight years of dedicated service to public education. She was the only Latino high-level elected official in the Washington area and holds the distinction of being the first Latina elected to this position in Maryland. Sol Gutiérrez has served as a member of the Board of Trustees of Capitol College, a small, private engineering college in Laurel, Maryland. She was twice elected Regional Vice-President of the Hispanic Caucus of the National School Board Association, a national education public policy organization. In January 1999, the Maryland State Teachers Association recognized her leadership in education with the MSTA Outstanding Service/ Politics Award.

Sol Gutiérrez began her professional career more than three decades ago after graduating with a Bachelor of Science in Chemistry from the Pennsylvania State University. She later received a Master of Science from American University in Scientific and Technical Information Systems/MIS and post-graduate studies in engineering at George Washington University. She is President and CEO of Sol Quality Systems, a small business enterprise that provides management consulting and systems engineering services, business process re-engineering, computer information systems, and applied technologies in education.

Before starting her company, she was a senior political appointee during the first term of the Clinton-Gore Administration. In 1994, Sol Gutiérrez received a political appointment from President Bill Clinton as the Deputy Administrator of the U.S. Dept. of Transportation's Research and Special Programs Administration. She directed the agency's safety, regulatory, and research and development programs, with oversight of major national transportation safety programs including Hazardous Materials Transportation Safety, Pipeline Safety, and Emergency Response.

As President of the Board of Directors of CASA de Maryland, Inc., a nonprofit organization serving the Latino new immigrant and low-income communities in Silver Spring and Takoma Park, Maryland, she is involved closely with issues of fair housing, adult education, immigration, and the provision of legal, health, and social services to those most in need in the new immigrant communities.

She has also served on numerous nonprofit boards such as the United Way, the Center for the Advancement of Hispanics in Science and Engineering Education, the Hispanic Council on International Relations, National Latino Communications Center, and Montgomery County Latino Civil Rights Task Force and the Hispanic Alliance. She served as the co-chair of the Latino Oversight Committee of The Smithsonian Institution from 1993–97.

As a nationally known Latina leader, *Hispanic Business Magazine* has twice recognized her among the "100 Most Influential Hispanics in U.S.A.," a distinction she received in 1996 and 1991. She is 1 of 12 Latino women selected for their significant contribution to American quality of life by the Bread and Roses Project: Women of Hope—Latinas Abriendo Camino. Their contributions appear in posters and educational materials widely distributed to schools, colleges, and community groups.

She received the Hispanic Achievement Award in Science from *Hispanic Magazine* and Apple Computer in 1993. She was featured in "Outstanding Women in Non-Traditional Careers" in *VISTA Magazine*. She is featured in two 1997 educational publications: *Latino Women of Science. Biographies, Experiments, and Hands On Activities* and *Women's Journeys, Women's Stories*.

Because of her community work, advocacy, and broad knowledge of issues impacting Latino communities, she is a regular guest on national and local Spanish-language TV and radio talk shows and can be heard as a commentator on education matters and Latino issues in and around Washington, D.C.

OSCAR RIOS (1950–)

Between 1971 and 1985, nine Latinos tried and failed to win election to the Watsonville City Council in Northern California. In the first district-based election in 1989, Oscar Rios, an immigrant from El Salvador, won the heavily Latino downtown residential District 1 seat. Oscar Rios was a labor activist who moved from San Francisco to Watsonville to help organize a strike of the city's frozen food industry. He was the first Latino council member elected in a district vote and was one of the first Salvadoran immigrants to be elected to public office in the United States.

In 1991, he became Watsonville's first Latino mayor. He helped changed the political structure in Watsonville by hiring more minorities in the municipal government and promoted bilingual services. He served as a council member in 1996 and was elected for a second term as mayor from 1998 and 2000.

LIZ FIGUEROA (1951–)

California State Senator Liz Figueroa, a Democrat, was re-elected to the California State Senate in November of 2002 to represent the 10th Senate District. Before her election she had served two terms in the California State Assembly. She is the first northern California Latina to be elected to the Legislature. She was born and raised in the San Francisco Bay Area. Her parents are both from El Salvador.

Senator Figueroa currently serves as the Chair of the Senate Committee on Business and Professions, the Joint Legislative Sunset Review Committee, the Senate Select Committee on International Trade Policy and State Legislation and the Senate Select Committee on Technological Crime and the Consumer. She is a member of the Senate Committees on Transportation, Health and Human Services, Insurance, Environmental Quality, and Industrial Relations. She also serves on the Senate Select Committees Bay Area Infrastructure, Bay Area Transportation, Economic Development, Health Care for All Californians, Defense and Aerospace Industry, and California's Horse Racing Industry.

Figueroa has been named Legislator of the Year by numerous organizations, including the March of Dimes, the American Academy of Pediatrics, the Association of Retarded Citizens, Leadership California, and the California National Organization for Women. The American Electronics Association named Figueroa Legislator of the Year three years in a row. In her first year with the Assembly, Figueroa delivered nine bills to the Governor's desk, all of which were signed into law—the highest percentage of any freshman legislator. Figueroa worked with the White House on landmark legislation that ensured a two-day hospital stay for mothers and their newborns, a bill that mirrored a successful California law Figueroa authored. In 1997, Figueroa co-chaired the conference committee that drafted California's Healthy Families program, which provides health insurance for the children of the working poor. Her work on behalf of women and human rights has gained international recognition. This includes such important issues as outlawing female genital mutilation, banning California's use of products made by slave labor, and prohibiting insurance companies from discriminating against victims of domestic violence.

As Senator, Figueroa has been a leader in the high-profile fight to reform managed care in California. Former governor Gray Davis characterized her bill giving patients the right to sue their HMO as the crown jewel in the HMO reform package and signed into law more HMO reform bills authored by Figueroa than by any other legislator. In addition, Figueroa's bill to protect the privacy of patient medical records makes California the nation's leader in guaranteeing confidential medical information is not abused by HMOs for any purpose not directly related to health care. Other legislation authored by Figueroa compelled insurance companies to replace child safety seats damaged in a collision, restricted false and misleading advertising for cosmetic surgery advertisements, and secured funding for the 410 mile-long San Francisco Bay Trail.

Senator Figueroa currently serves as a board member for the Mexican American Legal Defense and Educational Fund (MALDEF), Women in Government, Hispanic Community Affairs Council, Fremont Adult School Advisory Board, Lucile Packard Foundation for Children's Health, Legal Assistance for Seniors, California Corporate Board Registry Advisory Board, and the Board for the California Elected Women's Association for Education and Research (CEWAER). She also serves as Vice-Chair/President-Elect for the California Legislative Women's Caucus.

NELSON ARTIGA-DÍAZ

Nelson Artiga-Díaz has been director of the University of California San Francisco (UCSF) Family Dental Center for more than 15 years, and he played an important role in its founding during his days as a UCSF dental student. He graduated in 1975.

Under the leadership of Artiga-Díaz, volunteer dentists and dental students offer dental screenings for tooth decay, gum disease, oral cancer, and diabetes. The screenings are part of a larger mission that includes referrals for future care, patient education, research, and continued education for dentists. He is also very active in the fight against diabetes in the Latino community. Artiga-Diaz was recognized with the Chancellor's Award for Public Service.

As a student in 1971 and a self-described activist type, Artiga-Díaz appeared before the state General Assembly's Ways and Means Committee and argued for the establishment of a community clinic to serve needy patients. The funding for the center was provided then by the Chair of the Ways and Means at the time, Assemblyman Willie Brown, who went on to become San Francisco's mayor.

Artiga-Díaz was instrumental in the creation of the center, which today gets about 7,500 patient visits annually. About 85 percent of the patients are Latinos, nearly all of them are immigrants, and most of them receive care under the state's Denti-Cal program. The center had to close its doors in 2004 because of the budget crisis faced by California.

SYLVIA ROSALES-FIKE

Sylvia Rosales-Fike has a lifelong mission to help the poor and marginalized in society. Rosales-Fike is the founder of AnewAmerica Community Corporation in Berkeley, California, which trains those in need to help themselves. Immigrants enrolled in AnewAmerica's three-year program produce a business plan and learn accounting, pricing, and marketing, as well as how to build assets over time. They are required to be involved in activities that demonstrate social responsibility. While AnewAmerica works with micro-entrepreneurs to build their businesses, it guides them to better their communities, the environment, and the global society. Rosales-Fike has raised $2 million, built an infrastructure and capacity with 13 staff and a pool of professional consultants, and to date has served close to 400 new American families.

AnewAmerica grew as a concept while Rosales-Fike was a student at the John F. Kennedy School of Government at Harvard University. After graduation, she co-founded Community Bank of the Bay in 1994, the first commercial community development bank in California. The bank, which now has $40 million in assets, got its start through her assistance in raising $8 million. She went on to found AnewAmerica in 1999, with the goal of helping new Americans integrate themselves into their new adopted country.

Rosales-Fike came to the United States after her first husband was abducted and killed by the Salvadoran military because of the couple's work for the poor. Before the age of 30 and after being in this country less than one year, she became the executive director of the Central American Refugee Center (CARECEN) in Washington, D.C., an agency devoted to legal services and human rights work. She designed the nationwide "No Human Being Is Illegal" campaign with Nobel Laureate Elie Wiesel to raise awareness of the plight of refugees living in the United States.

She also served as the Director of the Center for Democracy in the Americas where she organized a series of behind-the-scenes/off-the-record conferences involving multiple stakeholders and bitter adversaries in the civil wars in El Salvador and Guatemala. The conferences were developed with the support and participation of leaders at the United Nations, the U.S. State Department, and Nobel Peace Laureate Oscar Arias.

ROBERTO LOVATO (1963–)

Roberto Lovato is a graduate of the University of California at Berkeley where he was a student activist interested in Central American and Latino immigrant issues. He took an active role in the Central American community in the San Francisco Bay Area but by the early 1990s he relocated in Los Angeles. He became the director of the Central American Resource Center (CARECEN) in Los Angeles where he was an advocate for Central American immigrant rights and services. By the late 1990s, he was a lecturer in the California State University Northridge (CSUN) and developed and taught a series of courses on the Central American experience in Southern California. He took the initiative and leadership to develop and propose an academic minor program in Central American Studies at CSUN.

The California State University at Northridge launched the first university Central American Studies program and academic minor in the country, aimed at serving a growing Central American population in Southern California that is projected to number more than 2.5 million by 2010. The minor program of study is offered through the university's College of Humanities, the groundbreaking project will develop courses, conduct research, and develop conferences covering a range of topics. The transnational/global approach adopted by the university's Central American Studies program has placed a major focus on the strong economic, cultural, and political relationships between the large Central American population in the United States and those in Central America. At the time of its creation, Lovato served as the first coordinator of the Central American Studies program.

Lovato has also served as president of the Los Angeles Human Relations Commission. He is the CEO of Lovato and Associates, a consulting firm that specializes in Latino marketing strategies in the United States. Lovato is also a writer for numerous news services and has had dozens of articles and commentaries of Latino issues published in a variety of newspapers and magazines.

DR. JUAN ROMAGOZA (1952–)

Physician Juan Romagoza grew up in Usulután in El Salvador. He followed the teachings and example of Archbishop Oscar Romero while attending

Juan Romagoza, Director of La Clinica del Pueblo, Washington, D.C. Photo by Carlos Texca.

medical school in San Salvador and began working to help the poor in El Salvador. He received his medical degree from the University of El Salvador in 1980. As a young doctor he provided free medical services to the rural poor. He was arrested under suspicion of being a guerrilla leader and tortured for 21 days, during which his fingers were cut to prevent him from practicing as a surgeon. He was released through the efforts of relatives and was smuggled into Guatemala and Mexico, and then into the United States with the help of the Sanctuary Movement.

In 1983, he went to San Francisco, where he worked as the Founder and Director of the Central American Refugee Committee. In 1986, he moved to Washington, D.C., and served as the Program Director for Casa del Pueblo and as Mental Health Counselor for La Morada Homeless Shelter. In 1987, he returned to San Francisco, where he served as the Director of Health Promoter Projects for the Good Samaritan Community Center and as the Director of Health Projects for the Central American Refugee Center. Dr. Romagoza returned to Washington, D.C., in 1988 to become the Executive Director of La Clinica del Pueblo, where he continues to serve the health care needs of the Latino community.

In 2002, he was part of a civil suit against a group of Salvadoran generals who had been implicated in ordering the violence and torture against him and others. The West Palm Beach, Florida, jury found the generals guilty and awarded him and the other plaintiffs the amount of $54.6 million dollars in damages.

Romagoza has received many awards and citations for his service to the community. Among the most notable are The Robert Wood Johnson Community Health Leadership Award, The International Center for Health Leadership and Development and University of Illinois at Chicago Leadership Award, La Raza Maclovio Barraza Leadership Award, and the Marcelino Pan y Vino Foundation Humanitarian Award.

CARLOS MAURICIO (1953–)

Educator and activist Carlos Mauricio was an agricultural engineering professor at the University of El Salvador. In 1983, he was asked to go out of his classroom for an emergency when he was abducted by a group of men. He was blindfolded and handcuffed and taken to the headquarters of the National Police. The police were convinced that he was a guerrilla member, and he was tortured for 10 days.

Carlos Mauricio still suffers the effects of the torture and his imprisonment and is able to express it in his poetry, testimony, and prose. He is very active

Carlos Mauricio. Photo by Carlos Texca.

in the Salvadoran immigrant community in the San Francisco Bay Area and is highly respected for his commitment to issues affecting Central American immigrants, local politics, and the arts. He was one of the plaintiffs in the trial against the Salvadoran generals in West Palm Beach. He is a speaker on Human Rights abuses and helped found an organization called "Alto a la Impunidad" (Stop Impunity), a coalition that helps survivors of torture get the services that they need to recover. He will fund the project with the 14 million dollars that he won in damages once the generals agree to pay.

Mauricio works as a high school science teacher. In 2003, the *San Francisco Bay Guardian* newspaper featured Carlos Mauricio in the Local Heroes category of the Best of the Bay section.

Appendix 2: Salvadoran Immigration to the United States by Year

Year	Numbers
2003	n/a
2002	n/a
2001	31,272
2000	22,578
1999	14,606
1998	14,590
1997	17,969
1996	17,903
1995	11,744
1994	17,644
1993	26,818
1992	26,191
1991	47,351
1990	80,173

(Continued)

(continued)

Year	Numbers
1989	57,878
1988	12,045
1987	10,693
1986	10,929
1981–1990	213,539
1971–1980	34,436
1961–1970	14,992
1951–1960	5,895
1941–1950	5,132
1931–1940	673

Data not reported separately until 1932.
Sources: Statistical Yearbooks of the INS, 1996–2001.

Glossary of Commonly Used Salvadoran Words

Salvadoran idioms (Salvadoreñismos) are extensive, many are humorous, but others are more vulgar. Some may have very strong sexual connotations but are often acceptable across the different social classes and in different situations. Many of the terms take grammatical liberties with the Spanish language, as Salvadorans tend to combine words together or abbreviate them as part of the combination of words. Many of the words used by Salvadorans originate in the Nahuat language used in the region before the arrival of the Europeans.

Ajolotado   Someone who is going around feeling very tense, desperate, hyperactive, or stressed out.

Baboso   Someone who acts dumb; often used to refer to any person, for example, *ese baboso*—that guy. Literally means someone who slobbers.

Barrios   Urban neighborhoods.

Bicha   Young girl; bug.

Bicho   Young boy; bug.

Cacaso   Things, objects, tools, or anything that has an inferior quality.

Camioneta   Bus, station wagon.

Campesino   Rural person, usually a farm laborer or seasonal agricultural worker.

Casamiento   Mixture of fried rice and beans, usually eaten for breakfast in El Salvador.

Chamba   Person named Salvador; also used to refer to a job or job site.

Chambiar   To work.

Chele   Light-skinned person.

Chévere   Expression that shows a sign of approval.

Chicharrón   Deep-fried pork meat and skin eaten with eggs, *pupusas,* or yucca.

China   Babysitter, nanny.

Chinear   To carry a baby or a load of things.

Chota   Police. Other terms used to identify the police are *La Tira, La Jura, los Cuilios.*

Choto   Usually expressed as *de choto*; for free. The movies are free today—*"El cine es de choto ahora."* I went all the way to look for Maria for nothing, she was not home—*"Hoy fui de choto hasta allá bien lejos a buscar a la María, y no estaba en su casa."*

Chucho   Dog. Also used to refer to an individual who does not like to share things or money.

Chumpa   Jacket; female turkey.

Chumpe   Turkey. Pan con Chumpe—a traditional Salvadoran sandwich with turkey meat, sauce, watercress, radishes, romaine lettuce, and curtido on a French roll.

Cipota   Young girl.

Cipote   Young child or boy.

Coyote   Smuggler who helps undocumented immigrants cross the U.S. border. Other names given include *pollero.*

Curandero   Traditional healer or shaman.

Cuche   Pig; something that is full; for example, The bus is full of people—*"La camioneta va bien cuche."*

Curtido   Mixture of cabbage, onions, carrots, oregano, and other spices that is pickled in vinegar and then eaten with pupusas or other Salvadoran foods.

Desmadre   Situation that is out of control and ends up in a disorderly fashion.

Encuchar   To be left in a tight spot.

Entendido   Health specialist.

Guanaco   Slang name for Salvadoran, commonly given to Salvadorans in Central America.

Guaro   Generic name given to any alcoholic beverage in El Salvador, but usually refers to hard liquor.

Güeviar   Stealing or appropriating something that is not one's own.

Guinda   *Salir en guinda* often refers to having to leave a place in a hurry or running from a dangerous situation.

Hacerse el loco   To play it dumb, to pretend not to pay attention to things.

Hacienda   Plantation.

Horchata   Traditional cold drink that is made from a variety of ground seeds and spices.

Ladino   Non-Indian person.

Loroco   Aromatic flower used as a condiment in Salvadoran cuisine, often added to cheese pupusas.

Mara   Street gang; group of friends. Another name used is *majada.*

Mareros   Street gang members.

Mascón   Game of soccer, basketball, or baseball.

Mestizo   Person of mixed Spanish and Indian blood.

Migra   U.S. immigration officials or the border patrol.

Mochila Backpack.

Mojado Undocumented immigrant. Other names used are *mojarra* or tilapia fish because the person had to swim the river to get across the border; and also *garrobo* or lizard because the person had to cross the border under the desert sun.

Mordida Bribe that has to be paid to government officials or to police to receive an illicit favor from the authorities, or paid to prevent a citation or fine to be given to a person.

Nana Mother.

Nel "No" or negative response.

Niña Little girl; a title often given to a woman as a sign of respect, for example, *la Niña Maria*.

Pisto Money.

Púchica Common expression of admiration or disgust. Used like "wow."

Pupusa National dish of El Salvador. Corn tortilla filled with cheese, pork, beans, or mixed. It is topped off with *curtido*. In some regions of El Salvador they may be made from rice flour rather than corn.

Pupuseria Restaurant that specializes in pupusas.

Remesas Remittances sent by Salvadoran immigrants to family in El Salvador.

Salvatrucha Slang name for Salvadorans.

Simón "Yes" or an affirmative answer.

Sióm Abbreviation of *Si Hombre* and affirmative response meaning "yes, man."

Susto Magical fright.

Tata Father.

Vapué Abbreviation of *vaya pués*, an affirmative response or sign of agreement.

Volado Almost anything or something that a person does not know the name of. For example, *"pasame ese volado,"* pass me that thing, or *"Voy a ir a hacer un volado,"* I am going to do something. Another word used with similar meanings is *Chunche*.

Yuca Sweet manioc root that is boiled or fried and typically eaten as an afternoon snack in El Salvador.

Bibliography

1999–2002 Yearbooks of Immigration Statistics (formerly entitled *Statistical Yearbook* of the Immigration and Naturalization Service).

American Civil Liberties Union. *Salvadorans in the United States: The Case for Extended Voluntary Departure*. Washington, D.C.: National Immigration and Alien Rights Project, Report No. 1, April 1984.

Amnesty International. *Annual Report*. Washington, D.C., 1983.

Amnesty International. "Extrajudicial Executions in El Salvador: Report of an Amnesty International Mission to Examine Post-mortem and Investigative Procedures." Amnesty International, 1984.

Boyd, Caroli, B. "Recent Immigration to the United States." In *Ethnic and Immigration Groups: The United States, Canada and England*, ed. P.J.F. Rosof, W. Zeizel, J. B. Quandt, and M. Maayan, 49–69. New York: Haworth Press, 1983.

Brzezinski, Mathew. "Hillbangers." *The New York Times Magazine* (August 15, 2004): 38–43.

Camarda, R. *Forced to Move: Salvadorean Refugees in Honduras*. San Francisco, Calif.: Solidarity Publications, 1985.

Central American Strategic Planning Committee. *Health Committee Strategic Plan*, project funded by the VESPER Society. Oakland, California, May 1995.

Córdova, Carlos B. "Organizing in Central American Communities in the United States." In *Community Organizing in a Diverse Society*, ed. Felix G. Rivera and John L. Erlich. Boston, Mass.: Allyn and Bacon, 1992.

———. "The Mission District: The Ethnic Diversity of the Latin American Enclave in San Francisco, California." *Journal of La Raza Studies* 2, no. 1 (Summer/Fall 1989): 21–32.

———. "Undocumented El Salvadoreans in the San Francisco Bay Area: Migration and Adaptation Dynamics." *Journal of La Raza Studies* 1, no. 1 (Fall 1987): 9–37.

———. "Migration and Acculturation Dynamics of Undocumented El Salvadoreans in the San Francisco Bay Area." PhD dissertation, University of San Francisco, 1986.

———. "The Role of Sorcery Prayers in El Salvador, Central America." Master's thesis, San Francisco State University, 1981.

Córdova, Carlos B., and Felix S. Kury. "Central American Mental Health Intervention Strategies." In *Latino Mental Health Perspectives in the United States*, ed. Alberto Lopez. Bethesda, MD: National Institute of Mental Health, Fall 1999.

Córdova, Carlos B., and Jorge del Pinal. *Hispanics-Latinos: Diverse Populations in a Multicultural Society*. Washington, D.C.: National Association of Hispanic Publications, 1996.

Córdova, Carlos B., and Raquel Rivera-Pinderhughes. "Central and South Americans." In *A Nation of Peoples: A Sourcebook on America's Multicultural Heritage*, ed. Elliott Barkan. Westport, Connecticut: Greenwood Press, May 1999.

Cresce, Arthur R., and Roberto R. Ramirez. *Analysis of General Hispanic Responses in Census 2000*. Working Paper No. 72. Population Division. Washington, D.C.: U.S. Bureau of the Census, 2003.

Culture Clash in America. http://www.cultureclash.com.

Deck, A. F. "Fundamentalism and the Hispanic Catholic." *America*, January 25, 1985.

———. "Proselytism and Hispanic Catholics: How Long Can We cry Wolf." *America*, December 10, 1988.

———. *The Second Wave: Hispanic Ministry and the Evangelization of Cultures*. New York: Paulist Press, 1989.

Fazlollah, M. "Fleeing Salvadorans: The Painful Journey North." *Migration Today*, XII, no. 2 (Summer 1984): 22–27.

Fitzpatrick, J. P. "The Importance of 'Community' in the Process of Immigrant Assimilation." *International Migration Review* I, no. 1 (Spring 1966): 5–16.

Gettleman, M. E., P. Lacefield, L. Menashe, D. Mermelstein, and R. Radosh, eds. *El Salvador: Central America in the New Cold War*. New York: Grove Press, 1981.

Gilbert, Lauren. *El Salvador's Death Squads: New Evidence from U.S. Documents*. Washington, D.C.: Center for International Policy, March 1994.

Gomez, Jorge Arias. *Farabundo Marti*. Editorial Universitaria Centroamericana (EDUCA), 1972.

Greeley, A. M. "Defection Among Hispanics." *America,* July 30, 1988.

Hamilton, Nora, and Norma Stoltz Chinchilla. "Central American Migration: A Framework for Analysis," *Latin American Research Review* 26, 1 (1991).

———. *Seeking Community in a Global City: Guatemalans and Salvadorans in Los Angeles*. Philadelphia, PA: Temple University Press, 2001.

Hayes-Bautista, David. "UCLA's Center for the Study of Latino Health and Culture." Report in "Study Compares 2 Latino Groups' Education Levels," by Patrick McDonnell. *Los Angeles Times*, February 24, 2004. http://www.cesla.med.ucla.edu/html/salvarticle.htm.

Lewis Mumford Center for Comparative Urban and Regional Research. *Hispanic Population and Residential Segregation*, University at Albany, State University of New York, 2004. http://mumford1.dyndns.org/cen2000/HispanicPop/HspPopData.htm.

Logan, John R. *The New Latinos: Who They Are, Where They Are*. Lewis Mumford Center for Comparative Urban and Regional Research, University at Albany, State University of New York, September 10, 2001.

Mahler, Sara. *American Dreaming: Immigrant Life on the Margins*. Princeton, N.J.: Princeton University Press, 1995.

Marin, Gerardo, and Gamba, Raymond. *Expectations and Experiences of Hispanic Catholics and Converts to Protestant Churches*. San Francisco: University of San Francisco, Social Psychology Laboratory, *Hispanic Studies*, February 1990.

Menjivar, Cecilia. *Fragmented Ties: Salvadoran Immigrant Networks in America*. Berkeley, CA: University of California Press, 2000.

Muller, Thomas, and Thomas Espenshade. *The Fourth Wave: California's Newest Immigrants*, Washington, D.C.: The Urban Institute Press, 1986.

National Lawyers Guild. *Immigration Law and Defense*. New York: Clark Boardman Company, 1981.

Orleans, Valerie. "Professor studies 'La Bajada' among L.A. Salvadorans. California State University at Fullerton." *Dateline*, February 5, 2004.

Padilla, A.M. "The Role of Cultural Awareness and Ethnic Loyalty in Acculturation, in *Acculturation: Theory, Models and Some New Findings*, ed. A.M. Padilla. Boulder, Colo.: Westview Press, 1980.

Portes, A., and R.L. Bach. *Latin Journey: Cuban and Mexican Immigrants in the United States*. Berkeley: University of California Press, 1985.

Portes, Alejandro, and Ruben G. Rumbaut. *Immigrant America: A Portrait*. Berkeley: University of California Press, 1990.

Public Health Service, U.S. Department of Health and Human Services. Healthy people 2000: National Health Promotion and Disease Prevention Objectives—full report with commentary (DHHS Publication No. (PHS) 91–50213). Washington, D.C.: U.S. Government Printing Office, 1990.

Ramirez, Roberto R., and G. Patricia de la Cruz. *The Hispanic Population in the United States: March 2002*, Current Population Reports, P20–545. Washington, D.C.: U.S. Census Bureau, 2002.

Ramos, George, and Tracy Wilkerson. "Unrest Widens Rift in Diverse Latino Population." *Los Angeles Times*, May 8, 1992, Metro Desk, part A, page 1, column 5.

Rodriguez, Richard. "For the Poor, Movement is the Only Answer to Natural Disasters." *JINN Magazine* 4, no. 23 (November 9–22, 1998).

Scudder, T., and Colson, E. "From Welfare to Development: A Conceptual Framework
      for the Analysis of Dislocated People. In *Involuntary Migration and Resettlement:*
      The Problems and Responses of Dislocated People, ed. A. Hansen and A. Oliver-
      Smith. Boulder, Colo.: Westview Press, 1982.

Tobar, Hector. "No Strength in Numbers for L.A.'s Divided Latinos." *Los Angeles*
      Times, September 1, 1992, Metro Desk, part A, page 1, column 1.

Triennial Comprehensive Report on Immigration. U.S. Department of Justice, April
      2002.

Vilar, J. J. D. "The Success of the Sects Among Hispanics in the United States."
      America, February 25, 1989.

Index

About the Author

CARLOS B. CORDOVA is Professor of Raza Studies at San Francisco State University.